Whitestone Hill

by Clair Jacobson

Pine Tree Publishing

La Crosse, 1991

Portions of this book were originally published in *North Dakota History* as "The Battle of Whitestone Hill" (Summer, 1977) and "A History of the Yanktonai and Hunkpatina Sioux" (Winter, 1980). This material is republished with permission from the State Historical Society of North Dakota.

Pine Tree Publishing
2510 Hass Street
La Crosse, WI 54601

Special thanks to Larry Remele, a friend and historian; to Iver Tveit for his long-time interest in what happened at Whitestone Hill; to Brenda and Bob Bradley for their contributions to the book; to my wife Gretchen and our children Kimberly, Heather, and Eric; and to Benjamin Franklin for pointing out that freedom of the press belongs to the person who owns a press.

Contents

Contents

Part 2: The Battle

Chapter 1

Buffalo Bones and a Battlefield

G athering buffalo bones by the wagonload provided extra income for many settlers on the Dakota frontier. These white, sun-bleached bones were hauled to the nearest town, loaded on railroad cars, and shipped to factories in eastern cities. There the bones were converted into phosphate for fertilizer and carbon for refining sugar. Buffalo bones were scattered across the Dakota prairie in such quantities that they became a "cash crop," a skeletal reminder of the vast herds of buffalo that once roamed the northern Great Plains.

Rediscovery of a Battle Site

On a fall day in the mid-1880's, a settler named Frank Drew was searching for buffalo bones in the low, rolling hills about nineteen miles northwest of the town of Ellendale in Dakota Territory. Drew had gathered and sold buffalo bones several times previously, but on this trip he accidentally discovered a spot with numerous bones that were not buffalo. The mass of skeletal remains Drew encountered that day included the heads of horses and mules. Scattered among these were reportedly human skulls and limb bones.

1

Other settlers in the area ventured to the site before all of the bones had been cleared away. In addition to the large number of bones from horses and mules, they found pans, copper kettles, a knife or dirk, and other indications that a significant conflict had taken place at this particular location. This was concluded to be the site of some type of battle that took place on the Dakota frontier long before settlers began arriving in the region in the early 1880's.[1]

A story about Frank Drew's discovery appeared in a local newspaper. Eventually the *St. Paul Pioneer Press* carried

Tom Shimmin was one of the first settlers to visit the Whitestone Hill site.

Photo from Shimmin-Tveit Museum, Forbes, ND

---

[1]J.C. Wilson to T.R. Shimmin, January 10, 1926, T.R. Shimmin Papers (Shimmin-Tveit Museum, Forbes, ND); R.M. Black, ed., *A History of Dickey County, North Dakota* (Ellendale, ND: The Dickey County Historical Society, 1930), pp. 271-72.

an article about finding the mass of bones in Dakota Territory, and J.C. Luce, a former soldier in the Iowa Cavalry during the Civil War, read the story. Luce traveled to the site, as did other ex-soldiers later, and helped identify it as Whitestone Hill. At that spot in September, 1863, United States cavalry troops had fought an important but relatively obscure battle with a large encampment of Indians.

More than 20 years before Frank Drew's discovery, U.S. cavalry troops led by General Alfred Sully had traveled into Dakota Territory hoping to locate and punish hostile Sioux Indians on the frontier, including Santee Sioux who had fled westward after taking part in the Minnesota Uprising of 1862. On September 3, 1863, Sully's troops discovered a large camp of about 3,500 Indians on the Missouri Coteau at a place the Indians called Whitestone Hill. A battle followed in which the Indians suffered severe losses in both lives and property.

Many of the Sioux Indians camped at Whitestone Hill were not Santees, however, but instead were members of the Yanktonai and Hunkpatina tribes. They were Indians who traditionally lived and hunted in this area of Dakota Territory, and in fact, were hunting buffalo and preparing the meat for winter when the soldiers discovered them.

A Place in History

Several of the Sioux or Dakota tribes, together with their influential leaders, have become well known through history and legend. The Hunkpapas with Sitting Bull, the Oglalas led by Red Cloud and later Crazy Horse, the Brule under Spotted Tail, and the Santees with the Mdewakanton leader Little Crow, are familiar names to many people. The Yanktonais and Hunkpatinas, however, have received little attention in history books, and have remained relatively obscure.

The battle at Whitestone Hill has likewise been given little notice in American frontier history, despite historian Elwyn

Robinson's observation that it was "the bloodiest ever fought on North Dakota soil."[2] This limited historical recognition of the Whitestone Hill battle is the result of the time and place at which the battle occurred, and not the significance of the event itself.

In 1863, the nation's attention was sharply focused on the Civil War. President Abraham Lincoln delivered his "Gettysburg Address" to dedicate a national cemetery on November 19, 1863. Lincoln's speech followed the battle at Gettysburg, Pennsylvania, which had been fought during the previous summer. It was also during the summer of 1863 that the first major military expeditions entered Dakota Territory. This went largely unnoticed by the American public. While the Indians and cavalry were engaged in Dakota Territory, Union and Confederate Armies were making headlines in the East, and this frontier conflict seemed insignificant by comparison.

At the time of the battle at Whitestone Hill, Dakota Territory had not yet been reached by the westward expansion of white settlers. Therefore this part of the frontier was totally devoid of a local white population that might have taken an interest in the event and left a written record. In addition, in 1863 communications from military units on the Dakota frontier were unavoidably slow in reaching the settlements in the East. Thus by the time the news reached the general population, it was already old news of a distant event.

Army-Indian Warfare

The 1863 engagement known as the Battle of Whitestone Hill has special significance when viewed in conjunction with subsequent Army-Indian conflicts on the western frontier.

During the fall of 1864, a group of Colorado volunteers, led by preacher-turned-soldier Col. John Chivington, attack-

---

[2]Elwyn B. Robinson, *History of North Dakota* (Lincoln: University of Nebraska Press, 1966), p. 101.

ed an Indian camp along Sand Creek in Colorado Territory. Although the Indians camped at Sand Creek were known to be peaceful Cheyennes, the soldiers surrounded the village and attacked anyway. Some 200 to 300 Indian men, women, and children were killed at Sand Creek. Among the survivors was a Cheyenne chief named Black Kettle. A government commission later investigated the attack at Sand Creek and sharply criticized the brutal work of the military. This engagement is known as the Sand Creek Massacre.[3]

During the winter of 1868, a group of U.S. Army soldiers led by Lt. Col. George Custer attacked an Indian camp along the Washita River in Indian Territory (present-day Oklahoma). Again these Indians were known to be peaceful, and again men, women, and children were killed in the unexpected assault. Between 40 and 100 Indians died at Washita in this attempt to destroy the village. Among the dead was Black Kettle, the same Cheyenne chief who had been at Sand Creek four years earlier. One historian, with a touch of irony, has labeled this engagement as "Custer's First Stand."[4]

During the summer of 1876, eleven weeks after "Custer's Last Stand" along the Little Bighorn in Montana Territory, one of the three armies sent to fight Indians that summer was making its way to the Black Hills in western Dakota Territory. These soldiers discovered an Indian encampment north of the Black Hills at a place called Slim Buttes. The soldiers attacked, 7 to 14 Indians were killed, and the camp was destroyed.[5]

Sand Creek in 1864, Washita in 1868, and Slim Buttes in 1876 represent a type of Army-Indian warfare that became

---

[3]Alvin M. Josephy, Jr., ed., *The American Heritage Book of Indians* (New York: American Heritage Publishing Co., 1961), pp. 345-46; Benjamin Capps, *The Indians* (Alexandria, VA: Time-Life Books, 1973), pp. 183-87; James A. Maxwell, ed., *America's Fascinating Indian Heritage* (Pleasantville, NY: The Reader's Digest Association, 1978), pp. 195-96.

[4]Josephy, pp. 346-47; Capps, pp. 190-91.

[5]Jerome A. Greene, *Slim Buttes, 1876* (Norman: University of Oklahoma Press, 1982), pp. 87-88, 92.

common on the western frontier, a method of warfare that had a devastating effect on the Indian way of life. When the 1863 Battle at Whitestone Hill is viewed in conjunction with these later engagements, its significance in the history of the American West becomes obvious. The Battle of Whitestone Hill in 1863 was one of the first major encounters west of the Mississippi River in which the Army severely crippled an Indian population by attacking and destroying a large Indian camp.

Yanktonai Turning Point

Whitestone Hill is symbolic of the cultural conflict between the Sioux Indians and white settlers. To the Sioux, it was essential that the wide open prairies and plains remain as they always had been. To the settlers, it was essential that these lands be opened up to settlement. Unfortunately, there was no compromise solution. And this led to violent conflicts such as the one at Whitestone Hill.

Whitestone Hill, to a large extent, also symbolizes the way of life of the Yanktonai and Hunkpatina Sioux who had long inhabited the eastern Dakota prairies. This book is the story of the Indians who lived and hunted at places like Whitestone Hill, and of the battle that helped bring an end to their traditional lifestyle.

Whitestone Hill is essentially divided into two parts. "Part 1: The Indians" – Chapters 2, 3 and 4 – is a history of the Yanktonai and Hunkpatina Sioux and describes their culture and traditional way of life on the prairies. "Part 2: The Battle" – Chapters 5, 6 and 7 – is a narrative of the events leading up to the conflict at Whitestone Hill and of the battle itself. This was a turning point in the history of the Yanktonai and Hunkpatina Sioux Indians, as is shown in the final chapter, "Road to Reservations."

Chapter 2

Waneta's People

The Yanktonai and Hunkpatina Indians belong to the Sioux or Dakota nation, a loose confederation of tribes that share a common ancestry, culture, language and location. The term "Dakota" means "allies" in the Santee dialect, while "Lakota" and "Nakota" have the same meaning in the Teton and Middle Dakota dialects.[1]

Seven Council Fires

While living in the Minnesota area in the 1600's, the Dakotas were organized into seven divisions or "council fires":[2]

1. Mdewakanton (Spirit Lake Village)
2. Wahpekute (Shooters Among the Leaves)

---

[1]John Upton Terrell, *American Indian Almanac* (New York: World Publishing Co., 1971), p. 271; C. Frank Turner, *Across the Medicine Line* (Toronto: Mc-Clelland and Stewart Ltd., 1973), p. 11.

[2]Ethel Nurge, ed., *The Modern Sioux* (Lincoln: University of Nebraska Press, 1970), pp. xii-xiii; Stephen E. Feraca and James H. Howard, "The Identity and Demography of the Dakota or Sioux Tribe," *Plains Anthropologist,* 8-20 (May, 1963), pp. 2-4.

7

3. Wahpeton (Dwellers Among the Leaves)
4. Sisseton (Fish Scale Village)
5. Yankton (End Village)
6. Yanktonai (Little End Village)[3]
   a. Yanktonai proper or Upper Yanktonai
   b. Hunkpatina (Campers at the Horn or End of the Camping Circle) or Lower Yanktonai[4]
7. Teton (Dwellers on the Plains)

The Dakotas spoke the Sioux[5] language and are often referred to as the Sioux Indians. This is somewhat misleading since a number of other tribes, including the Biloxi who lived in what is now the state of Mississippi and the Catawba who lived in the Carolinas, also spoke the Siouan language. The name Dakota, based on political and cultural ties between the seven "council fires," may be more correct. When used here, however, the words "Dakota" and "Sioux" will be synonymous, with "Sioux" referring only to the Dakota Sioux Indians.

---

[3]Spellings of tribal names vary from source to source. The Yanktonai, for example, are also referred to as "Ihanktonwana," "Yanktoanan," "Yanctonie," "Yankton Ahna," and so on. Frederick Webb Hodge, ed., *Handbook of American Indians North of Mexico*, 2 Parts (New York: Pageant Books, Inc., 1960), Part I, p. 991; Nurge, p. xiii.

[4]"Hunkpatina" should not be confused with "Hunkpapa," the name of one of the tribes of the Teton division. Both names refer to the "hunkpa" or ends of a tribal circle. Hunkpapa is also written Uncpapa, Oncpapa, and so on. The name Hunkpatina is sometimes shortened to "Hunkpati." James Owen Dorsey, "Siouan Sociology," in *Fifteenth Annual Report of the Bureau of Ethnology, 1893-'94*, ed. by J.W. Powell (Washington: Government Printing Office, 1897), p. 221; Edward A. Milligan, *Dakota Twilight: The Standing Rock Sioux, 1874-1890* (Hicksville, NY: Exposition Press, 1976), p. 99; Jan M. Dykshorn, "William Fuller's Crow Creek and Lower Brule Paintings," *South Dakota History*, 6-4 (Fall, 1976), p. 418.

[5]The name Sioux comes from a French corruption of the Chippewa word "Natowesiwok" (also spelled "Nadowe-is-iw") which means "snakes" or "enemies." The Chippewas, traditional enemies of their Dakota neighbors, referred to them as such. Early French traders, encountering the Chippewas earlier than the Dakotas, thought the word sounded like "Nadouessioux," and this was abbreviated to "Sioux." Wesley R. Hurt, *Sioux Indians II: Dakota Sioux Indians* (New York: Garland Publishing Inc., 1974), p. 6; Feraca and Howard, p. 2; Nurge, pp. xii, 215; Terrell, *American Indian Almanac*, p. 271.

The Dakota Indians were living in the Minnesota area when Europeans first heard about them around 1640, and they had undoubtedly been living there for many years.[6] There are several theories about earlier locations of the Dakotas and their migration to the central Minnesota area, but since there are no written records to confirm the theories, the early history of these Indians remains unknown.

Four of the Dakota tribes, the Yankton, Yanktonai, Hunkpatina, and Assiniboin, "lived in the thickly timbered region surrounding the headwaters of the Mississippi."[7] The Hunkpatinas and Assiniboins[8] were originally part of the Yanktonai tribe. While these four Dakota tribes appear to have descended from a single ancestral tribe, it is not known whether the Yankton or the Yanktonai was the elder tribe. These Indians occupied the Leech Lake region north of Mille Lacs.[9]

---

[6]John Upton Terrell, *Sioux Trail* (New York: McGraw-Hill Book Company, 1974), p. 178.

[7]David I. Bushnell, Jr., *Villages of the Algonquian, Siouan, and Caddoan Tribes West of the Mississippi*, Smithsonian Institution Bureau of American Ethnology, Bulletin 77 (Washington: Government Printing Office, 1922), p. 54.

[8]The Assiniboins had already broken away and moved north where they allied themselves with the Algonquin Cree when the Sioux were first mentioned in the *Jesuit Relation* in 1640. Originally members of the *Wazikute* band of the Yanktonai, the Assiniboins were called "Hohe" (Rebels) by the Dakota. The name "Assiniboin" means "Cook-with-stones people" in the Algonquin language. The break between the Assiniboins and their fellow tribesmen has been variously attributed to "two women who quarreled over the division of a buffalo," a strong desire by the Assiniboins "to improve their economy," and "family feuds arising from the seduction of a woman." Terrell, *Sioux Trail*, p. 180; Robert H. Lowie, *The Assiniboine*, (New York: American Museum of Natural History, 1909), p. 7; W.J. McGee, "The Siouan Indians," in *Fifteenth Annual Report of the Bureau of Ethnology, 1893-'94* (Washington: Government Printing Office, 1897), p. 161; Royal B. Hassrick, *The Sioux: Life and Customs of a Warrior Society* (Norman: University of Oklahoma Press, 1964), p. 59.

[9]James H. Howard, "The Wiciyela or Middle Dakota," *Museum News* (Vermillion: University of South Dakota, July-August, 1966), p. 1;
Edward S. Curtis, *The North American Indian*, 20 Vols. (Cambridge, MA: The University Press, 1908), Vol. 3, p. 121; Terrell, *Sioux Trail*, p. 180.

Moving Westward

The Teton Dakotas, also living in the Mille Lacs region of central Minnesota, were the first of the Dakota tribes to begin a westward migration, and appear to have reached the Lake Traverse area by 1700.[10] They were followed by the Yanktons who migrated in a southwesterly direction, and the Yanktonais and Hunkpatinas who began their westward movement in the latter part of the 1600's.[11] The Santees remained in Minnesota and occupied the St. Peter's (or Minnesota) River area.

The westward movement of Dakota tribes appears to have come partially as a result of pressures from their traditional enemies, the Chippewa (Ojibwa), who had received firearms from white traders at an earlier date. The availability of large numbers of buffalo on the prairies provided another incentive for the Dakotas to move south and west.[12]

As Dakota tribes moved west, changes in location and population made a different breakdown of the Dakota nation more appropriate. The Mdewakanton, Wahpekute, Wahpeton and Sisseton tribes remained in the Minnesota area west of the Mississippi River and became collectively known as the Santee or Eastern Dakotas. The Yanktons and Yanktonais comprised the Middle Dakotas and lived west of the Santees, toward the Missouri River. The Teton or Western Dakotas inhabited the plains area from the Missouri River west to the Rocky Mountains, and were broken down into seven tribes: 1) Blackfoot, 2) Brule, 3) Hunkpapa, 4) Minneconjou, 5) Oglala, 6) Sans Arc, and 7) Two Kettle.[13]

---

[10]James H. Howard, "The Teton or Western Dakota," *Museum News* (Vermillion: University of South Dakota, September-October, 1966), p. 1.

[11]Feraca and Howard, p. 3.

[12]Feraca and Howard, p. 2; Hassrick, p. 59.

[13]Jamake Highwater, *Indian America* (New York: David McKay Co., 1975), p. 319; Nurge, pp. xii-xv; Turner, pp. 11-12; Terrell, *American Indian Almanac*, pp. 270-71.

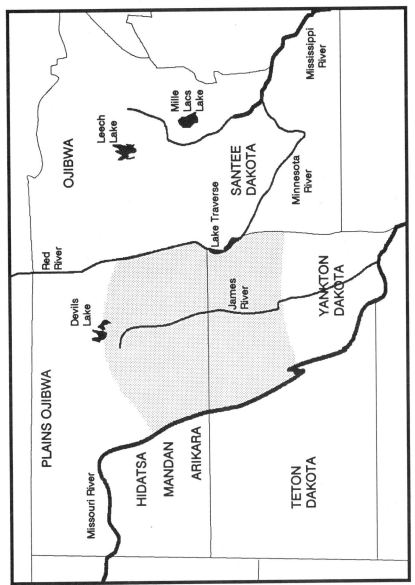

This shows the approximate territory occupied by the Yanktonai Dakota during the 1800-1850 period. Leech Lake and Mille Lacs Lake are included to show the area from which they gradually moved westward, and the present state borders have been added as a reference.

11

Early white traders and explorers who had contact with the Yanktonai and Hunkpatina tribes generally failed to differentiate between them, and referred to them collectively as Yanktonais. Because the contact between the whites and these Indians was so limited, and because the two tribes were so closely related historically and culturally, it is probable that many of these white people did not realize that there were actually two distinct tribes inhabiting this region.

When whites did differentiate between the two tribes in the 1800's, they often referred to the Yanktonais as Upper Yanktonais because they lived north of the Hunkpatinas, primarily in what is now southeastern North Dakota. The Hunkpatinas, on the other hand, became known as the Lower Yanktonais, and primarily inhabited the northeastern part of what is South Dakota today.[14] It is therefore not surprising that the name Hunkpatina has remained obscure, and that the two tribes are often referred to collectively as Yanktonais.

The Yanktonai and Hunkpatina tribes were divided into the following subdivisions or bands:[15]

Yanktonai
1. *Wazi-kute:* "Shooters-among-the-pines"
2. *Takini:* "Improved-in-condition" (as a lean animal)
3. *Cikcitcena (Siksicena):* "Bad ones of different sorts"
4. *Bakihon:* "Gash themselves with knives"
5. *Kiyuksa:* "Breakers of the law or custom"
6. *Pabaksa:* "Cut heads"
7. (Name forgotten)

Hunkpatina
1. *Pute-temini:* "Sweat lips"
2. *Cuniktceka:* "Common dogs"
3. *Takhuha Yuta:* "Eaters of hide scrapings"

---

[14]Terrell, *Sioux Trail*, p. 181.

[15]Alan R. Woolworth, "Ethnohistorical Report on the Yankton Sioux," in *Sioux Indians III* (New York: Garland Publishing Inc., 1974), pp. 8-9; Dorsey, "Siouan Sociology," p. 218; Howard, "The Wiciyela or Middle Dakota," p. 8.

4. *Sanona:* "Shoot at some white object"
5. *Ihasa:* "Red lips"
6. *Itegu:* "Burnt faces"
7. *Pteyutecni:* "Eat no buffalo cows"

The Cutheads

The Cutheads, one of the bands of Yanktonai, became particularly significant during the 1800's. It is possible that the Cutheads actually broke away from the Yanktonais and functioned as a separate tribe. James McLaughlin, a government Indian inspector and Indian agent, said that they got the name Cutheads after a fight which occurred when they seceded from the Yanktonais, adding that "their leader sustained a scalp wound and the name Cut Head was given them at once and accepted without protest or question."[16] This may or may not have been the case, but it is clear that the Cutheads (or *Pabaksa*) became quite influential. Reports by military officers after the battle of Whitestone Hill, for example, specifically identified the Cutheads as being at the Indian camp,[17] and the United States government signed a separate treaty with the Cutheads in 1868.[18]

Edwin Thompson Denig, a trader at Fort Union who had lived on the upper Missouri River for 23 years, wrote about the Sioux Indians in 1855 and stated that after 1840 the Yanktonais had "become separated into three distinct bands

---

[16]James McLaughlin, *My Friend the Indian* (Boston: Houghton Mifflin Company, 1910), p. 25.

[17]U.S. Department of War, *The War of the Rebellion: A Compilation of the Official Records of the Union and Confederate Armies*, Series I (Washington: Government Printing Office, 1880-1902), Vol. XXII, Part I – Official Records, pp. 558, 567. (Hereafter referred to as *Official Records*.)

[18]Charles J. Kappler, ed., *Indian Affairs: Laws and Treaties*, Vol. II (Treaties), (Washington: Government Printing Office, 1904), p. 1007.

each having its own ruler." He identified these bands as "the *Tete Coupees, Gens des Perches* and *Gens des Pins*."[19] This reinforces the possibility that the Cutheads actually functioned as a separate tribe, since the Hunkpatinas were also called the *Gens de perche* or "people of the pole," and the Cutheads were also known as the *Tete Coupe*.[20] In his "General Classification of the Sioux," Denig listed the *Tete Coupees* as "Pah Baxah" (*Pabaksa*) and the *Gens des Pin* as "Wahzecootai" (*Wazi-kute*).[21]

Waneta, the Charger

The increased prominence of the Cutheads may have come through the influential Cuthead leader, Waneta (also spelled "Wanotan," "Wah na ton," "Wahnaataa," and so on). Waneta was born along the Elm River (in what is today northwestern Brown County, South Dakota) around 1795.[22] He was the son of Red Thunder, a Cuthead chief who favored the English in the War of 1812, and in the spring of 1813 both Waneta and his father joined the English forces. He was at the siege of Fort Meigs and the battle of Fort Stephenson, and at the latter place he received the name Waneta, "he who charges his enemies" or "the charger." Waneta was given a

[19]Edwin Thompson Denig, *Five Indian Tribes of the Upper Missouri*, ed. John C. Ewers (Norman: University of Oklahoma Press, 1961), pp. 29-30;
Report of Harry H. Anderson, "Before the Indian Claims Commission: Docket No. 74: Sioux Nation, et al. v. United States of America." (The place and date of preparation are not indicated. The South Dakota State Historical Society at Pierre has a copy of this report.); Hurt, *Sioux Indians II*, pp. 202-203;

[20]Woolworth, p. 9; Anderson, pp. 19-20.

[21]Hurt, *Sioux Indians II*, p. 203.

[22]N. Jane Hunt, ed., *South Dakota Historical Markers* (Sioux Falls, SD: Brevet Press, 1974), p. 26.

captain's commission by the British as a result of his valor, and at Sandusky he received several wounds.[23]

Although still a young man, Waneta became a prominent Cuthead chief following the War of 1812. He continued to favor the British over the Americans until 1820, and then changed his preference after an attempt to capture Fort Snelling by stealth had failed.[24]

In 1823 a government expedition led by Stephen Long visited Waneta's camp near Lake Traverse. William Keating, the historian for the expedition, referred to Wanotan (Waneta) as "the most distinguished chief of the Yanktoanan tribe" and provided the following description:

> Those who know him well, commend his sagacity and judgment, as well as his valour. He is a tall man, being upwards of six feet high; his countenance would be esteemed handsome in any country, his features being regular and well-shaped. There is an intelligence that beams through his eye, which is not the usual concomitant of Indian features. His manners are dignified and reserved; his attitudes are graceful and easy, though they appear to be somewhat studied.[25]

Keating and the other members of the group appear to have been quite impressed by the chief and to have considered him very influential among the Yanktonais. After leaving Lake Traverse to travel north to Pembina, the leaders of the expedition again called on Waneta:

> Vague reports of large parties of Dacotas had been circulated for some days past, and a rumour that five

---

[23]William H. Keating, *Narrative of an Expedition to the Source of St. Peter's River*, 2 Vols. (Minneapolis: Ross & Haines, 1959), Vol. I, p. 448; Doane Robinson, *A History of the Dakota or Sioux Indians* (Minneapolis: Ross & Haines, 1967), pp. 86-87, 101; Hodge, p. 910; Denig, pp. 31-32.

[24]Hodge, p. 910; Doane Robinson, pp. 103-104.

[25]Keating, Vol. I, pp. 448-49.

Waneta in 1823

Artists created portraits of Waneta on at least four separate occasions. Charles Bird King reportedly captured Waneta's likeness in 1823, and since the above drawing bears that date in Doane Robinson's *History of the Dakota or Sioux Indians*, it is probable that this is King's work. George Catlin painted Waneta at Fort Pierre in 1832, and it appears likely that the painting on page 17 (also published in Robinson's book) was done by Catlin. Both pictures share elements characteristic of all portraits of Waneta, such as the bear claw necklace and the nine sticks worn in his hair to symbolize the nine wounds he received while fighting for the British during the War of 1812.

Waneta, the Charger

hundred lodges of the Yanktoanan were collected on Shienne River made us desirous of being accompanied by Wanotan, which he readily agreed to do; finding, however, that these reports were groundless, and that this excursion would be inconvenient to him, as it would deprive him of the opportunity of laying in a store of buffalo meat for winter, we reluctantly acquiesced in his wish to be released from his promise.[26]

On July 5, 1825, Waneta signed a treaty of trade and intercourse with the Americans at Fort Pierre, and by August 17, 1825, he had traveled to Prairie du Chien and signed a treaty which fixed the boundaries of Sioux territory.[27]

Edwin Thompson Denig, a fur trader, did not write as favorably about Waneta as Keating had, although even Denig chose to refer to him as "decidedly the greatest Indian chief of modern times." Denig went on to describe the chief:

Strongly supported by extensive family connections, decided and brave in his actions, and feared on account of his supposed supernatural protection, his word was law and his people his slaves. Dressed in officer's clothing, top boots, green spectacles, sword and pistols, his strange appearance contrasted greatly with that of his half clad followers.[28]

According to Denig, Waneta's dealings with fur traders included extracting "high pay" from them before allowing them to deal with his tribe, and forcing his entire tribe to pay

---

[26]Keating, Vol. II, pp. 2-3.

[27]The fact that Waneta signed the two treaties in such a short time span at such widely separated locations is impressive in itself. Fort Pierre (located on the Missouri River in what is today South Dakota) and Prairie du Chien (along the Mississippi River in present-day Wisconsin) are over 450 miles apart by the most direct route. Waneta undoubtedly had to travel much farther using rough trails and water routes between the two places, yet he made the trip in less than a month and a half.

[28]Denig, p. 32.

for items which had been stolen from the trader earlier by only "a few scoundrels . . . . By such examples as these he brought his people to respect his orders and by killing one or two of his band, to fear his vengeance."[29]

Waneta died around 1840[30] near the mouth of the Warreconnee (the present Beaver Creek in Emmons County, North Dakota).[31] Denig believed it was following Waneta's death that the Yanktonai and Hunkpatina separated into three groups, the *Gens des Perches*, *Gens des Pins*, and *Tete Coupees*.[32]

[29]Denig, pp. 32-33.

[30]Doane Robinson stated that Waneta died in 1848, but this appears to be an error. Two contemporaries of the chief listed his death around 1840: Edwin Thompson Denig, a fur trader, said he died in 1840; and Stephen Riggs, a missionary, referred to him as "the late Wanatan" in his 1840 account. Doane Robinson, p. 106; Denig, p. 30; Anderson, pp. 19-20.

[31]Hodge, p. 910.

Chapter 3

Traders and Explorers Arrive

The white fur traders, missionaries, explorers and adventurers who first encountered the Yanktonai and Hunkpatina Indians provided a chronology of these tribes in their written accounts. Through their journals, memoirs, expedition logs, government reports and letters, they presented an interesting, although somewhat limited, picture of the Yanktonais and Hunkpatinas during the two centuries that preceded the creation of Sioux Indian reservations in the 1860's.

French Traders and Explorers

The first recorded contacts between white men and the Dakota or Sioux Indians were by missionaries and explorers who did not identify individual tribes. In 1640 a Jesuit priest from French Canada wrote that Jean Nicolet had learned about the "Naduessiu" from the Winnebagoes, and in 1642 two Jesuit missionaries, Charles Raymbaut and Issac Jogues, learned from the Chippewas that the "Nadouessis" lived about eighteen days journey west of Sault St. Marie.[1]

Radisson and Grosseilliers, two French traders, were probably the first Europeans to make contact with the Sioux when they traveled into central Minnesota around 1661. Among the Sioux tribes which they saw were the "Nadoneseronons" or "Nation of the Beefe" who hunted buffalo on the prairie during the summer and spent the winter in the northern woods.[2] A map made by Father Louis Hennepin in 1683 indicated the location of the Sioux tribes in Minnesota and placed the "Hanctons" (Yankton-Yanktonai) north and east of two lakes which apparently were Leech Lake and Lake Winnibigoshish.[3]

In 1700 Charles Pierre Le Sueur, a French explorer, traveled up the Mississippi and Minnesota rivers to the mouth of the Blue Earth River (near present day Mankato, Minnesota) where he hoped to mine copper ore. He established a trading post, and while there he collected some detailed information about the Sioux tribes, dividing them into the "Scious of the East" and the "Scious of the West." The "Scious of the East" have been identified as the Santee division, and two groups of Santees also appear to have been listed among the "Scious of the West."[4] Although there is some difficulty in identifying the various tribes listed by Le Sueur, it appears that the "Tintangaoughiatons" were the Tetons and the "Hinanetons – Village of the Red Stone Quarry" were the Yanktons. This indicates that the Yanktons had moved from the Mille Lacs area where Hennepin had seen them to the Pipestone Quarry area.[5]

---

[1]Anderson, p. 4; Hurt, *Sioux Indians II*, pp. 44-45.

[2]Hurt, *Sioux Indians II*, pp. 46-47.

[3]J.M. Gillette, "The Advent of the American Indian into North Dakota," *North Dakota Historical Quarterly*, 6-3 (April, 1932), p. 218; Hurt, *Sioux Indians II*, p. 52.

[4]Doane Robinson, p. 43; Hurt, *Sioux Indians II*, pp. 60-61.

[5]Hurt, *Sioux Indians II*, p. 61.

Le Sueur also included the "Touchouaesintons – Village of the Pole" among the "Scious of the West," and this apparently refers to the Hunkpatina, since they were also known as the "Gens de Perche" or "people of the pole." Another tribe from this list, the "Ouasicoutetons – Village of those who shoot into a great pine," has been classified as the Wazikute or pine shooters band of the Yanktonai,[6] but this tribe may have been the Wahpekute (or Wazikute) tribe of the Santee division instead of the Wazikute band of the Yanktonai.

Pierre La Verendrye, a French-Canadian trader and explorer, traveled southwest from the Assiniboine River in Canada to visit the Mandans living along the Missouri River in 1738. Although he does not appear to have encountered the Sioux, the Assiniboin Indians who traveled with him warned of the danger of Sioux attacks as they neared the Mandan villages. The Mandans also mentioned the Sioux after LaVerendrye arrived, indicating that either the Tetons or the Yanktonais were traveling and raiding as far west as the upper Missouri River at that time.[7]

Two of La Verendrye's sons, Louis and Francois, traveled to the Mandan villages and beyond in 1742-43, and on April 9, 1743, they visited a village of about 20 lodges of the "Gens de la Fleche Collee" or "Sioux of the Prairies," probably on the east bank of the Missouri between the Cheyenne and Grande rivers. These Indians were probably Tetons.[8]

While the earliest accounts of the Sioux Indians were written by French traders, explorers and missionaries, this began to change after the Treaty of Paris in 1763. In this treaty France ceded her possessions west of the Mississippi River to Spain and those east of the river to England. The Europeans

---

[6]Anderson, p. 4.

[7]"Distribution of North Dakota Indian Tribes," *The Museum Review*, 1 (State Historical Society of North Dakota, November, 1946), p. 5; Hurt, *Sioux Indians II*, p. 72.

[8]Hurt, *Sioux Indians II*, pp. 74-75, 90.

who visited the Sioux during the next 30 years were therefore representing British and Spanish interests for the most part.

Peter Pond, British Fur Trader

In the winter of 1774-75, Peter Pond, a British fur trader and explorer, visited a large group of Indians in Minnesota "who ware Nottawaweas By Nation But the Band was Cald Yantonose."[9] These Indians were camped along a river "about two Hundred Miles" above his winter camp on the St. Peter's (Minnesota) River. Pond, one of the earliest Englishmen to visit these Indians, said that "thay Never Saw a trader Before On thare One Ground or at Least Saw a Bale of Goods Opened."[10]

> Ye Yantonose are faroshas and Rude in thare Maners Perhaps Oeing in Sum masher to thare Leadi[n]g an Obsger [obscure] life in the Planes. Thay are not Convarsant with Every other tribe. Thay Seldom Sea thare Nighbers. Thay Leade a wandering Life in that Exstensive Plane Betwene the Miseurea & Missicippey.[11]

Pond described the "Leather tents" used by the Yantonose, and then continued his account of their semi-nomadic life style:

---

[9]There may be some question as to whether these "Yantonose" Indians were Yanktons or Yanktonais. Charles M. Gates edited "The Narrative of Peter Pond" in *Five Fur Traders of the Northwest* and identified the Yantonose as Yanktons. Frank Gilbert Roe in *The Indian and the Horse*, on the other hand, concluded that these Indians were Yanktonais. Harry H. Anderson, in his report "Before the Indian Claims Commission," also identified them as Yanktonais. It is therefore probable that the Indians Pond visited were Yanktonais, and not Yanktons, but since the two tribes apparently were closely related at the time, Pond's descriptions may have been appropriate for either tribe.

[10]"The Narrative of Peter Pond," Charles M. Gates, ed., *Five Fur Traders of the Northwest* (Minneapolis: University of Minnesota Press, 1933), pp. 52, 55.

[11]*Ibid.*, p. 58.

Thay Have a Grate Number of Horses and Dogs which Carres thare Bageag when thay Move from Plase to Plase. Thay Make youse of Buffeloes dung for fuel as there is but little or no Wood upon the Planes. Thay are Continuely on the Watch for feare of Beaing Sarprised By thare Enemies who are all Round them. Thare war Implements are Sum fire armes, Boses and arroes & Spear which thay have Continuely in thare hands.[12]

The Yantonose relied on the buffalo for numerous aspects of their existence. The buffalo provided meat and hides, as well as the dung with which they built their fires. In addition, Pond mentioned that he was fed "a Sort of Soope thick and with Pounded Corn Mele" which was served in a "Dish which was Bark & the Spoon Made out of a Buffeloes Horn." Horses were used while hunting buffalo:

Thay Run down the Buffelow with thare Horses and Kill as Much Meat as thay Please. In Order to have thare Horseis Long Winded thay Slit thair Noses up to the Grissel of thare head which Make them Breath Verey freely. I Have Sean them Run with those of Natrall Nostrals and Cum in Apearantley Not the Least Out of Breath.[13]

Pond went on to briefly describe the burials, beliefs and marriages of the Yantonose:

These when a parson dies among them in winter thay Carrea the Boddey with them til thay Cum to Sum Spot of Wood and thay Put it up on a Scaffel till when the frost is out of Ground thay Intare it. Thay Beleve in two Sperits – one Good & one Bad. Thay Genaley Get thare wife By Contract with the Parans. Thay are

---

[12]"The Narrative of Peter Pond," p. 58.

[13]*Ibid.*, pp. 54, 58-59.

Verey Gellas of thare women. It Sumtimes Hapens that a Man will take his Nighbers Wife from him But Both are Oblige to Quit the tribe thay Belong to But it is Seldum that you can Hear of Murders Committed among them.

Pond added that he "Seldum Hurd of thefts among themselves whatever thay Mite Due to others."[14]

In the 1790's fur traders from St. Louis made voyages up the Missouri River and left accounts of having encountered Sioux Indians. Jacques D'Eglise made trips in 1791 and 1793, Jean Trudeau made a voyage in 1794, and James Mackay traveled up the Missouri in 1795.[15] All three left information about encounters with the Sioux, but the Yanktonais were not specifically mentioned.

The Louisiana Purchase of 1803 again brought changes in the contacts between whites and the Dakota or Sioux Indians. After the United States purchased the Louisiana Territory from France (who had reacquired it from Spain in 1800), American explorers were commissioned to travel through the area, making notes on the country and its inhabitants.

Lewis and Clark Expedition

Meriwether Lewis and William Clark, the first American explorers to travel up the Missouri River, met "Sceoux or Dar co tar" bands on their 1804-06 journey.[16] After the expedition had returned, Clark talked with Nicholas Biddle who took notes which included a list of the Sioux or Dakota tribes.

---

[14]"The Narrative of Peter Pond," p. 59.

[15]Hurt, *Sioux Indians II*, p. 61; Anderson, pp. 6-9.

[16]Reuben Gold Thwaites, ed., *Original Journals of the Lewis and Clark Expedition, 1804-1806*, 8 Vols. (New York: Arno Press, 1969), Vol. 1, p. 132.

Biddle's list of ten tribes appears to have included the Yanktonais, who were described as:

> Yanktons of the plains or Big devils who rove on the heads of the Scioux, Jacques & Red river about 500 men.[17]

Zebulon Pike, American Explorer

In 1805 Zebulon Pike explored the upper Mississippi region for the United States and identified the Yanktonais as "the Yanctongs of the north, . . . headed by a chief called Muckpaanutah," in his list of the Sioux tribes:

> This band are never stationary, but with the Titongs are the most erratic bands of all the Sioux, sometimes to be found on the borders of the Lower Red River, sometimes on the Missouri, and on those immense plains which are between the two rivers.[18]

Pike mentioned the Yanctongs in various entries in his journal, not indicating whether he was writing about Yanctongs of the north (Yanktonais) or Yanctongs of the south (Yanktons). On one occasion Pike learned from another Indian "that the bands of the Sussitongs and Yanctongs had actually determined to make war on the Chipeways, and that they had formed a party of 150 or 160 men . . . ." On another occasion, Pike talked with "*Red Thunder*, chief of the Yanctongs, the most savage band of Sioux," and learned that a trader named Murdoch Cameron was selling rum at Red Thunder's village.[19] In this case, it

---

[17]Donald Jackson, ed., *Letters of the Lewis and Clark Expedition, with Related Documents, 1783-1854* (Urbana: University of Illinois Press, 1962), pp. 497, 536.

[18]Zebulon Montgomery Pike, *Sources of the Mississippi and the Western Louisiana Territory* (Ann Arbor, MI: University Microfilms, Inc., 1966), app. to Part I, pp. 60-61.

[19]*Ibid.*, pp. 50, 101.

appears that Pike was referring to Waneta's village, since his father, Red Thunder, was a Cuthead chief during this period.

Pike said the eastern bands of Sioux dealt with traders from Michilimackinac, and that one of these bands supplied "the Yanctongs of the north, and Titongs, with the small quantities of iron works which they require. Fire arms are not in much estimation with them." Pike also provided an interesting description of the nomadic life style of the Yanctongs and Titongs:

> The Yanctongs and Titongs are the most independent Indians in the world; they follow the buffalo as chance directs; clothing themselves with the skin, and making their lodges, bridles, and saddles of the same materials, the flesh of the animal furnishing their food. Possessing innumerable herds of horses, they are here this day, 500 miles off ten days hence, and find themselves equally at home in either place, moving with a rapidity scarcely to be imagined by the inhabitants of the civilized world.[20]

In 1812 Manuel Lisa led a party up the Missouri River to establish trading posts for the Missouri Fur Company. One of the posts was built on the east side of the Missouri (near present day Chamberlain, South Dakota) for a trader named Bijou who would trade with "the Yentonas, Tetons and Shaunee."[21] The Yentonas have been identified as Yanktonais and the Shaunee as Saones.[22]

---

[20]Pike, p. 62.

[21]Anderson, p. 12.

[22]The term "Saones" was sometimes used to designate five of the Teton tribes, the Minneconjous, Hunkpapas, Sans Arcs, Blackfeet and Two Kettles. The Brules and Oglalas were the first to apply the term to the other five Teton tribes, and it still appeared in reports by traders and explorers in the 1830's. The usage of "Saones" seems to have varied somewhat, however, with the Minneconjous being excluded in some cases and small sub-bands of the Upper and Lower Yanktonais being called Saones in others. Anderson, p. 2; Hurt, *Sioux Indians II*, p. 203.

American exploration and fur trade along the upper Missouri River came to a halt with the outbreak of hostilities between the United States and England in the War of 1812. During this period the British gained the support of many of the Indians in the upper midwest and on the northern plains, including Waneta and his father. Indian support for the British prevented Americans from traveling and trading among these tribes, and American contact with the Sioux Indians did not resume until the early 1820's.

William Keating and the Dog Feast

One of the most detailed early accounts of the Yanktonais was compiled by William Keating, a member of the Stephen Long expedition sent out by the U.S. government in 1823. This account was later published as the *Narrative of an Expedition to the Source of the St. Peters's River.* Long's expedition traveled through the Minnesota region to Lake Traverse and then down the Red River to the international boundary with Canada. Among the tribes encountered were the Yanktonais, whom Keating called "Yanktoanan":

> Yanktoanan, (the Fern Leaves.) This is one of the most important tribes, as its population amounts to one-fifth that of the whole nation. They have no fixed residence, but dwell in fine skin lodges, well dressed and decorated. Their hunting grounds are very extensive, spreading from Red river to the Missouri. They frequent, for purposes of trade, Lake Travers, Big Stone Lake, and the Shienne river. Their principal chief is Wanotan, (the Charger,) .... [23]

Keating also mentioned the "Yanktoan" (Yankton), translated the name as "descended from the Fern leaves," and

---

[23]Keating, Vol. I, pp. 403-04.

This drawing of Waneta and his son was originally published in the 1825 edition of William H. Keating's *Narrative of an Expedition to the Source of the St. Peter's River.* Engraved in London by R. Fenner after the completion of the Stephen H. Long expedition, the drawing may have been based on a written description, and it is probable that the artist had never seen an American Indian.

stated that they "are in every respect similar, and probably separated from" the Yanktoanan.

The Long expedition arrived at Waneta's camp near the Columbia Fur Company's post at the mouth of Lake Traverse on July 23, 1823, and immediately received an invitation to a feast prepared by the Indians.[24] Three dogs had been killed in preparation for the festival, and a pavilion had been "erected by the union of several large skin-lodges. Fine buffalo-robes were spread all around, and the air was perfumed by the odor of sweet scented grass which had been burned in it."

As soon as we had taken our seats, the chief passed his pipe round, and while we were engaged in smoking, two of the Indians arose and uncovered the large kettles which were standing over the fire: they emptied their contents into a dozen wooden dishes which were placed all round the lodge; these consisted of buffalo meat boiled with tepsin, also the same vegetable boiled without the meat, in buffalo grease, and finally, the much esteemed dog meat, all of which were dressed without salt. In compliance with the established usage of travellers to taste of every thing, we all partook of the latter with a mixed feeling of curiosity and reluctance. Could we have divested ourselves entirely of the prejudices of education, we should doubtless have unhesitatingly acknowledged this to be one of the best dishes that we had ever tasted: it was remarkably fat, was sweet and palatable: it had none of that dry stringy character which we had expected to find in it, and it was entirely destitute of the strong taste which we had apprehended that it possessed.[25]

Despite the facts that dogs were used by the Yanktonais as beasts of burden and that dog meat was considered a

---

[24]Doane Robinson, p. 104.

[25]Keating, Vol. I, p. 450-52.

delicacy reserved for special occasions, dogs were thought to have a sacred character:

> We were warned by our trading friends that the bones of this animal are treated with great respect by the Dacotas; we, therefore, took care to replace them in the dishes; and we are informed, that after such a feast is concluded, the bones are carefully collected, the flesh scraped off from them, and that after being washed, they are buried in the ground, partly, as it is said, to testify to the dog-species, that in feasting upon one of their number no disrespect was meant to the species itself, and partly also from a belief, that the bones of the animal will rise and reproduce another.[26]

When General Henry Atkinson and Major Benjamin O'Fallon concluded the 1825 treaties with Missouri River tribes, their report included the following information about the Yanktonais:

> The Yanctonies are also a roving band of the Sioux and range in the intermediate country between the Missouri and the river St. Peter's, embracing the headwaters of the river Jacques. They also hunt the buffalo, whose flesh is their principal means of subsistence, and their skins, with those of the elk and deer, their raiment. They live in leather lodges, which they move at pleasure; are well armed with fusees, and supplied with horses and a few mules. They are estimated at four thousand souls, of which eight hundred are warriors; friendly to the whites, and enemies to all Indians but the tribes of their own nation. Their trading ground is also on the river Jacques.[27]

---

[26]Keating, Vol. I, p. 452.

[27]Anderson, p. 14; Hurt, *Sioux Indians II*, p. 176.

Prince Maximilian and Karl Bodmer

A German prince, Maximilian of Wied-Neuwied, came to America in 1832 to study the plains Indians.[28] He traveled up the Missouri River, spent the winter of 1833-34 at Fort Clark (northwest of the present city of Bismarck, North Dakota), and mentioned the "Yanktonans" in various entries in his journal. Accompanying Maximilian on the trip was a young Swiss artist, Karl Bodmer, whom Maximilian had recruited to draw and paint portraits and scenes of Indian life. The January 21, 1834, entry in Maximilian's journal includes the following:

> Three Yanktonans came to the fort with a view to persuade the Mandans to join in an expedition against another tribe. Mr. Bodmer took a very excellent likeness of Psihdje-Sahpa, one of the three Yanktonans.[29]

Psihdje-Sahpa "came often to Maximilian's quarters to roast ears of corn in the fireplace during the bitterly cold weather of January."[30] Bodmer's portrait of Psihdje-Sahpa is shown on page 35.

Frontier Contact Increases

As the American frontier was pushed westward during the 1800's, Indian agents, fur traders, missionaries and military men were increasingly in contact with the plains Indians, and the Yanktonais appear in their records and reports more and more often. Only a few of these will be mentioned here.

---

[28]Josephy, p. 262.

[29]Reuben Gold Thwaites, ed., *Early Western Travels, 1748-1846*, Vol. 24, Maximilian's Travels (Cleveland, OH: The Arthur H. Clark Company, 1906), pp. 61-62.

[30]Davis Thomas and Karin Ronnefeldt, eds., *People of the First Man* (New York: E.P. Dutton & Co., Inc., n.d.), p. 193.

33

Lawrence Taliaferro's 1839 report, submitted after 20 years as Sioux agent on the Mississippi, included information about the Yanktonais:

> This is the most populous tribe of Sioux within this agency, and have at times been troublesome on the plains, and may be rated at 2150 souls. They depend on the buffalo for subsistence and raiment to a very great extent, as they trade but very little anywhere and roam in the country on Red river of the north and its tributaries, and upon those of the Missouri, and reside with others at certain seasons at the "Devil's Lake," beyond the Cheyenne River of the north. One or two seasons past the small pox was quite destructive among these people; upwards of 60 lodges perished by that loathsome disease.[31]

Stephen Riggs, a Protestant missionary from the St. Peter's River area of Minnesota, traveled to Fort Pierre in 1840 and talked with Indians and old traders there. In his account of the trip, Riggs stated that the Yanktonais "now range to Devil's Lake and the Missouri and even beyond that river."

> Riggs recorded that the chief band of the Yanktonais was the Hunkpatidan, consisting of 200 lodges, and "generally are found in the country east of the Missouri. The other bands comprehended under this general name (Yanktonais) are the Pabakse (Tete Coupe or Cut Heads), of whom the late Wanatan was the chief; the Wazikute (shooters in the pine) and the Kiyuksa; all estimated at 200 lodges. These go as far north as Devil's Lake and frequently pass beyond the Missouri."[32]

---

[31]Anderson, p. 19.
[32]*Ibid.*, pp. 19-20.

Psihdje-Sahpa

Psihdje-Sahpa, a Yanktonai Sioux, was painted by the Swiss artist Karl Bodmer at Fort Clark along the Missouri River during the winter of 1833-34. This is perhaps the best portrait of a member of the tribe.

Photo from Joslyn Art Museum, Omaha, Nebraska

General William S. Harney spent the winter of 1855-56 at Fort Pierre, and while there he talked with almost all of the Missouri Sioux bands. His list of these bands included:

10. 1st Band of Yanktonais – "Two Bears" Chief. Their country, from James to Mouse Rivers, the east side of the Missouri River, and now near the mouth of "Long Lake" – about 180 miles from here.

11. 2nd Band of Yanktonais – "Don't Eat Buffalo" ("Nobsedie") Chief. Their country, about the "Bone Butte" near the head of James River, about 150 miles from here.

12. 3rd Band of Yanktonais – "Big Head" Chief. Their country, from here to mouth of Mouse River, now about 40 miles below Fort Clarke, on Missouri River, at "Apple Creek."

13. 4th Band of Yanktonais – "Medicine Bear" or "Cut himself" Chief. Their country, from here to the mouth of Mouse River, on the East Bank of the Missouri – now about 250 miles from here.[33]

Lieutenant G. K. Warren, the topographical engineer with the Harney Expedition, traveled extensively on the plains and provided the following description of the Yanktonais in his 1858 report:

Inhantonwannas (Yanktonnas):
meaning one of the "End Village" bands. They range between James River and the Missouri, as high north as Devil's Lake, number about 800 lodges .... They suffered severely from the ravages of the small-pox in the winter of 1856 and 1857. A small portion, under a

[33] Anderson, pp. 22-23.

chief called Little Soldier, live in dirt lodges during the summer.[34]

The accounts by Harney and Warren are particularly interesting in view of the 1863 battle at Whitestone Hill. Four of these Indian chiefs have been specifically identified as being part of the Whitestone Hill encampment. In his official report of the battle, General Sully mentioned both "the notorious chief Big-head" and Little Soldier, who had "the reputation of being a 'good Indian'."[35] Colonel Robert Furnas wrote in his journal that "Medicine Bear's Band" was among the Indians camped at Whitestone Hill.[36] Two Bears has been identified as a leader at the camp in other sources.[37] General Harney and Lieutenant Warren, in their accounts of the Sioux Indians in 1855 and 1858, identify all four of these chiefs as leaders in the Yanktonai and Hunkpatina tribes.

---

[34]Hurt, *Sioux Indians II*, pp. 227-28.

[35]*Official Records*, p. 558.

[36]Richard D. Rowen, ed., "The Second Nebraska's Campaign Against the Sioux," *Nebraska History*, 44-1 (March, 1963), p. 24.

[37]Aaron McGaffey Beede, *Heart-in-the-Lodge* (Bismarck, ND: Bismarck Tribune Co., 1915), pp. 5, 8; "Whitestone Battlefield: A History from 1863 to 1976" (Prepared by the Whitestone Battlefield Celebration Committee, 1976), pp. 3-4.

Chapter 4

Horses, Tipis, and Buffalo

As they moved west from the Minnesota woods onto the Dakota prairies, the Yanktonai and Hunkpatina tribes developed a semi-nomadic life style largely dependent on the buffalo. They rode horses, lived in tipis that could be easily moved, and hunted the plentiful buffalo. By the mid-1800's, the two tribes had a combined population of about 6,000.[1] A

---

[1]The population of the Yanktonai and Hunkpatina Indians prior to the reservation era can be approximated through the estimates of white men who came into contact with them. Lewis and Clark, in 1806, estimated the number of men at 500, which Frederick Webb Hodge equated to a population of about 1,750. The estimate of the Long expedition in 1823 was 5,200. Denig said that in 1833 there were 400 lodges of Yanktonais (*Pah Baxah*, 250 lodges; *Wahzecootai*, 100 lodges; and *Gens des Perches*, 50 lodges), but he did not convert this to a population figure. Henry Rowe Schoolcraft placed the population in 1852 at 6,000 (including 600 lodges and 1,800 men). Warren's 1856 estimate was 6,400. In 1857, W.J. Cullen, Superintendent of Indian Affairs in Minnesota, reported the number of Yanktonai lodges at 450, plus about 200 lodges of Cuthead Yanktonais. In August 1864, General Henry Sibley estimated that bands of Yanktonais totaling 1,000 lodges and 6,000 people were camped in the Devils Lake region. The accuracy of these estimates probably varied with the time period and the source, but it seems apparent that the Yanktonai and Hunkpatina tribes had a combined population of about 6,000. Hodge, pp. 990-91; Hurt, *Sioux Indians II*, p. 202; Henry Rowe Schoolcraft, *History of the Indian Tribes of the United States*, 6 Vols. (Philadelphia: J.B. Lippincott & Co., 1857), Vol. 6, p. 695; Anderson, pp. 25, 31.

population of 6,000 Indians would be approximately 600 lodges.[2]

Neighboring Tribes

The culture of the Yanktonai Indians was similar, in many respects, to that of the other tribes inhabiting the northern plains in the 1700's and 1800's. In many ways they resembled their Dakota neighbors on the plains, the Tetons to the west and the Yanktons to the south, as a result of their similar origin, language and location, and because they sometimes shared hunting territory and acted as military allies.

There were also cultural differences between the plains tribes, however. It has been pointed out that "no single description of the culture of the Dakota Sioux can be given that would hold true for all the tribes or for any single tribe over a long period of time."[3] As the Yanktonais moved west from the central Minnesota area, they left a woodland environment for the "tall grass" or prairie country east of the Missouri River (as opposed to the "short grass" or high plains west of the Missouri).[4] This change in location brought with it changes in life style.

-----

[2]Since population figures were often reported in terms of lodges rather than people, and since the average number of Indians dwelling in a lodge is seldom given, Thaddeus Culbertson's observations shed some light on this subject. During an expedition up the Missouri River in 1850, Culbertson concluded that there were about 3,000 lodges containing a population of about 30,000 Sioux Indians in that area. He explained further that "the average souls per lodge has been put at ten, on the authority of Mr. Picotte, who has had every opportunity of making a correct estimate. He thinks that eight souls per lodge might not be too low, but he prefers to put the estimate at ten."
Thaddeus A. Culbertson, *Journal of an Expedition to the Mauvaises Terres and the Upper Missouri in 1850*, ed. John Francis McDermott, Smithsonian Institution Bureau of American Ethnology, Bulletin 147 (Washington: Government Printing Office, 1952), p. 132.

[3]Hurt, *Sioux Indians II*, p. 13.

[4]Howard, "Middle Dakota," p. 1.

While moving west toward the Missouri River, the Yanktonais encountered the Caddoan speaking Arikara and the Siouan speaking Mandan and Hidatsa tribes. James Howard, a noted authority on the Middle Dakota Indians, has stated that "much of the subsequent cultural change on the part of the Yankton and Yanktonai can be explained in terms of their contacts, both warlike and friendly, with these semi-sedentary riverine groups." Both the Yanktonais and the Yanktons borrowed from the culture of these tribes who "were already well adapted to the Missouri River Valley environment and that of the adjacent region to the east." These cultural changes by the Yanktonais and Yanktons were to such a degree that Howard concluded that "in their economy, housing, dress, and ceremonial, the Middle Dakota sometimes resembled the other Missouri Valley tribes more closely than the Eastern or Western divisions of their own people."[5]

The changes made by the Yanktonais as they moved from the central Minnesota woodlands to the Dakota prairies were similar to those made by other tribes also moving to the plains, including the Chippewas, Cheyennes and other Dakotas. Historian Elwin Robinson summarized these changes:

In the forest, they were expert canoemen, ate fish and wild rice, built bark-covered wigwams, boiled maple sap into sugar, wore soft-soled moccasins, and used long bows. These customs were well suited to the forest and lake country of Minnesota, but the grassland was far different. . . . In their new home they rode horses, ate buffalo meat and tipsin roots, slept in skin tipis, made sugar from box-elder sap, wore hard-soled moccasins, and hunted with short bows.[6]

[5]Howard, "Middle Dakota," p. 1.

[6]Elwyn B. Robinson, *History of North Dakota* (Lincoln: University of Nebraska Press, 1966), pp. 26-27.

Horses and Buffalo

The acquisition of horses was an essential part of this transition to the plains environment. The Yanktonais had horses when Peter Pond visited them in the 1770's and appear to have acquired them a short time earlier.[7] Horses enabled them to travel great distances in a relatively short period of time, provided transportation for their tipis and other camp equipment, gave them an advantage over sedentary tribes in warfare, and kept them abreast of running buffalo during their hunts.

The Yanktonais went on two buffalo hunts each year, in mid-summer and late fall. Herds containing tens of thousands of buffalo grazed between the Mississippi and Missouri Rivers. The Yanktonais also crossed to the west side of the Missouri River for some of their hunts.[8] The huge number of buffalo roaming the plains is evident from the estimate by General William T. Sherman that between the Mississippi River and the Rocky Mountains there were 9,500,000 buffalo.[9]

The most common method of hunting buffalo involved two groups of hunters on horseback charging the herd from different directions in a coordinated attack. Each hunter killed as many buffalo as possible during the chase. Other members of the tribe followed behind the hunters to butcher the buffalo that had been killed.[10]

After the buffalo had been slaughtered, the hides and slices of meat were carried back to the camp. Dogs harnessed with travoises, two trailing poles fastened over their shoulders and separated by a platform of sticks, were also used to

---

[7]Frank Gilbert Roe, *The Indian and the Horse* (Norman: University of Oklahoma Press, 1955), pp. 182, 191.

[8]Howard, "Middle Dakota," p. 1.

[9]Clement A. Lounsberry, *North Dakota: History and People* (Chicago: S.J. Clarke Publishing Company, 1917), pp. 33-34.

[10]Hassrick, pp. 176-77; Lounsberry, pp. 34-35.

transport the meat.[11] Some of the buffalo meat was preserved for later use by making pemmican:

> The meat was cut into long strips from half an inch to an inch in thickness, and these were hung on racks to dry, with a slow fire built under them in order to smoke them a little. When dried and smoked slightly, they were placed on the flesh side of a buffalo hide, and whipped until beaten into shreds, and then mixed with hot tallow in large kettles. Poured into sacks while soft, the thick, pliable mass became so hard that it often required a heavy blow to break it. It could be eaten without further preparation, or could be cooked with vegetables and in various ways. If handled properly it could be kept for many years perfectly pure and sweet.[12]

Keating left a similar description of this process, and added that "sometimes, in order to give it a pleasant taste, it is mixed with a sort of wild cherry, which is pounded and introduced, stone and all." He said that when heated in a pan, pemmican "is equal to the best hashed meat."[13]

The Yanktonais also jerked buffalo meat to preserve it. The meat was cut in long thin slices and hung over poles to dry in the sun. Keating said that "two days of exposure to a hot sun are sufficient to dry the meat so that it will keep."[14]

In addition to jerked meat and pemmican, the buffalo provided fresh meat, and served as a source of sinews for thread, strings for bows, horns and bones for implements, paunches for vessels, ropes for tethering animals, and skins for tipis, clothing, carpets and bedding.[15]

---

[11]Keating, Vol. 2, pp. 5-6.

[12]Lounsberry, pp. 35-36.

[13]Keating, Vol. 1, p. 447.

[14]Keating, Vol. 2, p. 7.

[15]Lounsberry, p. 32; Hurt, *Sioux Indians II*, p. 19.

Buffalo did not provide the only source of meat for the Yanktonais, however, as Howard pointed out:

> Bison, elk, deer and antelope were hunted throughout the year by individuals and small groups, but this sort of hunting was done closer to the home villages, and east of the Missouri. Small game was taken with rabbit sticks, shaped something like a boomerang ....[16]

The Yanktonais fished with large seines made of willow branches and weighted with stones. These were moved along a river or stream by wading men who brought the ends of the seine together periodically and speared the trapped fish. They also used fish traps, and the hook-and-line and bow-and-arrow methods of fishing.[17]

These Indians gathered tipsina (described as a nutritious wild turnip), chokecherries, and other wild foods, and grew their own crops of corn, squash and beans.[18]

Tipis and Earthlodges

Three types of dwelling were used by the Yanktonais: the skin-covered wikiup, the skin tipi, and the earthlodge. The wikiups, generally used only by poor families, were dome-shaped and elongated, and covered with hides, bark or mats. The tipis were conical and of the standard three-pole foundation type.[19] In 1833 Maximilian described the tipis used by Yanktons or Yanktoans (Yanktonais):

---

[16]Howard, "Middle Dakota," pp. 1-2.

[17]*Ibid.*, p. 2.

[18]Paul Beckwith, *Notes on Customs of the Dakotahs* (Ext. Smithsonian Institute Report, 1886, Facsimile Reproduction, Seattle, WA: Shorey Book Store, 1970), pp. 254-55; Howard, "Middle Dakota", p. 2.

[19]Howard, "Middle Dakota", p. 2.

Like other Plains Indians, the Yanktonai and Hunkpatina preserved fresh meat by "jerking" (sun-drying), and by mixing it with berries to make pemmican. Tons of the meat were dried annually and served as a major staple of the diet. This camp scene was drawn by Ernest Henry Griset for the Bureau of American Ethnology and appeared in *Bulletin 77* (1927).

The tents of the Sioux are high pointed cones, made of strong poles, covered with buffalo skins, closely sewed together. These skins are scraped on both sides, so that they become as transparent as parchment, and give free admission to the light. At the top, where the poles meet, or cross each other, there is an opening, to let out the smoke, which they endeavor to close by a piece of the skin covering of the tent, fixed to a separate pole standing upright, and fastened to the upper part of the covering on the side from which the wind blows. The door is a slit, in the front of the tent, which is generally closed by another piece of buffalo hide, stretched upon a frame.[20]

In addition to the wikiups and tipis, four Yanktonai earthlodge villages have been located, two of them along the Missouri River (near Fort Yates, North Dakota, and Fort Thompson, South Dakota). A third village was along the James River near the present Ashton, South Dakota. The fourth and most well known Yanktonai earthlodge village was at Armadale Island, northeast of Melette, South Dakota, along the James River. This is often referred to as Drifting Goose's village, named after a Lower Yanktonai (Hunk-patina) chief.[21]

One of these "Dirt Lodge" villages, apparently Drifting Goose's village,[22] was described by historian George W. Kingsbury:

There were fifteen of these lodges. They were located in a large circle, 165 feet in diameter, with playgrounds attached, and a medicine pole and lookout station in

---

[20]Bushnell, Bulletin 77, p. 58.

[21]Howard, "Middle Dakota," p. 3.

[22]Wesley R. Hurt, "House Types of the Santee Indians," *Museum News* (Vermillion: University of South Dakota, December, 1953), pp 1-3; James H. Howard, "Drifting Goose's Village," *Museum News* (Vermillion: University of South Dakota, January, 1954), p. 2.

the center .... The lodges were constructed by placing sticks of wood five feet long upright in the ground, binding their tops together with long poles, then placing other poles on this structure and leaning their tops to the center, forming the roof. The entire structure was then covered with sod from the base to the summit, leaving a small smoke-hole at the apex of the roof. The lodges were not all of the same dimensions; some would accommodate seventy-five Indians, others about twenty-five.[23]

Kingsbury said the Indians had built a large fish trap in the nearby James River in 1863. He described the farming conducted near the village: "Forty acres of land had been broken up nearby in Indian fashion, and the squaws cultivated at least one-half of it to corn; they also raised beans, peas and turnips, potatoes, and possibly other vegetables."[24] Howard concluded that "the Yanktonai earthlodge was very likely derived from the Mandan or Arikara in the early part of the nineteenth century," adding that "it resembled the lodges of these two tribes in nearly all respects."[25]

In 1856 Alfred J. Vaughan, agent for the upper Missouri tribes, reported that "a portion of the Yanctonais, headed by the 'Little Soldier', have built a permanent village on the left bank of the Missouri, about one hundred miles below Fort Clarke." This village appears to have been located on the east bank of the Missouri above the mouth of Spring Creek, near the present Pollock, South Dakota.[26]

---

[23]George W. Kingsbury, *History of Dakota Territory* (Chicago: S.J. Clarke Publishing Co., 1915), Vol. 1, pp. 306-07.

[24]*Ibid.*

[25]Howard, "Middle Dakota," p. 3.

[26]Anderson, p. 24.

Weapons and Clothing

The Yanktonais used the short bow for both hunting and warfare since it was well suited for use on horseback. Keating observed that Waneta's bow did not exceed "four feet in length; the arrows were proportional." The Yanktonais also had firearms when Keating visited them in 1823. He mentioned that during a dance put on for his party each performer used the wing of a bird to "beat time on his gun, arrow or something that would emit a sound." These Indians also used stone-headed warclubs and soft hide armor and shields.[27]

The tools and implements used by the Yanktonais were made from various materials including bone, wood, iron and stone. Both bone and iron scrapers were used to clean the flesh and hair off hides before tanning. Tools with stone heads and wooden handles were used for pounding. Mortars for grinding were made both from wood and the skin of a buffalo's head. The Yanktonais used bullboats, adopted from the Arikara, Mandan and Hidatsa, for traveling on rivers. They made baskets, parfleches and small pottery vessels.[28]

Yanktonai men wore fringed buckskin shirts similar to those of the other plains Indians. Their breechcloths were "of the 'riverine' style, tucked in over the belt for a few inches in back and hanging out over the belt for about a foot in front." Their leggings differed from the common plains style of beaded strips up the sides by displaying bead and quill designs in the front at the bottom of the leg. Howard described the hair ornamentation common among the men:

> Yanktonai men wore their hair in three braids, two at the sides of the head and a third, wrapped in otter fur, hanging down the back. In front the hair was worn in bangs, leaving a longer lock hanging over the brow and nose. At either side of the forehead hourglass shaped

---

[27]Howard, "Middle Dakota," p. 5;   Keating, Vol. 2, p. 8; Vol. 1, p. 457.
[28]Keating, Vol. 1, p. 447; Vol. 2, p. 7;   Howard, "Middle Dakota," pp. 3, 5.

ornaments of dentalium shells sewn on rawhide were tied to the hair, with pendants of dentalium shells hanging as far as the shoulders. Fur turbans were worn by some men, and the warbonnet was used to some extent.[29]

Yanktonai women wore one-piece dresses which often included "an additional cape-like piece completely covered with dentalium shells." Their moccasins had a high buckskin top or leg-wrap, similar to those used by women of the riverine tribes. Heavy necklaces of vertical bone "hair pipes" were worn by the women.[30]

When the Long expedition visited Waneta's camp in 1823, the chief decided to pay them a formal visit on one occasion, and he therefore dressed accordingly. Keating left an excellent description of this formal clothing, and wrote that "we have never seen a more dignified looking person, or a more becoming dress."

> The most prominent part of his apparel was a splendid cloak or mantle of buffalo skins, dressed so as to be of a fine white colour; it was decorated with small tufts of owls' feathers, and others of various hues . . . . A splendid necklace, formed of about sixty claws of the grizzly bear, imparted a manly character to his whole appearance. His leggings, jacket, and moccassins, were in the real Dacota fashion, being made of white skins, profusely decorated with human hair; his moccassins were variegated with the plumage of several birds. In his hair he wore nine sticks neatly cut and smoothed, and painted with vermilion; these designated the number of gunshot wounds which he had received; they were secured by a strip of red cloth; two plaited tresses of his hair were allowed to hang

---

[29]Howard, "Middle Dakota," p. 4.

[30]*Ibid.*

forward; his face was tastefully painted with ver-
milion: in his hand he wore a large fan of feathers of
the turkey, which he frequently used.[31]

Yanktonai Society

The social structure of the Yanktonais appears to have
changed as they adapted to a semi-nomadic life style on the
prairie. At one time the Yanktonais apparently were divided
into clans, since clan taboo names such as *Pteyutecni* (Eat no
buffalo cows) and *Kiyuksa* (Breakers of the law or custom)
were used by some of the bands, but the clan system was
discontinued. In the bands, the principal social unit beyond
the family was the sub-band, each of which had its own name
and often constituted a village group.[32]

Each band was governed by a chief and a council. Chief-
tainship tended to be hereditary, with the chief's eldest son or
some other male heir succeeding the chief in the event of
death. This rule was not always followed, however. The chief
and council were assisted by police, and this group was increased to form a "soldiers lodge" in times of war or other
emergency. Among the Sioux, "the power of the chief was
nominal, depending more upon his prestige and other per-
sonality traits than upon traditional authority."[33]

Marriage among the Yanktonais generally involved a man
paying goods to his future wife's parents. Peter Pond mentioned this practice around 1775, and it continued into the
early 1900's.[34]

---

[31]Keating, Vol. 1, pp. 455-56.

[32]Howard, "Middle Dakota," p. 3.

[33]Howard, "Middle Dakota," pp. 3-4; Hurt, *Sioux Indians II*, p. 14.

[34]Howard, "Middle Dakota," p. 6; "The Narrative of Peter Pond," p. 59.

Waneta, Leader of the Cutheads

By Artist J.O. Lewis – Photo from Library of Congress

It is apparent that the buffalo played a dominant role in the economy of the Yanktonais. In addition, at least some bands were engaged in agriculture for part of their subsistence. Following the arrival of white men, the fur trade also became a significant factor in their economy.

Fur Trade

The Columbia Fur Company was formed in 1822, largely by former employees of the Northwest Company which had merged with the Hudson Bay Company in 1821. The company established a base at Lake Traverse which was ideally located between the heads of the Red and St. Peter's rivers, while Fort Tecumseh (near the present Pierre, South Dakota) served as its principal establishment on the Missouri River. The Columbia Fur Company also built subsidiary posts between Lake Traverse and the Missouri to trade with the Yanktonais. One of these, the Colin Campbell Fur Post, was located along the Elm River, near its junction with the James, to handle the trade with Waneta's band of Cutheads. Buffalo and beaver skins appear to have made up a significant portion of this trade. In 1827, the Columbia Fur Company united with John Jacob Astor's American Fur Company and continued to function under a new title, the Upper Missouri Outfit.[35]

A number of fur trading posts were built and maintained in the upper Missouri River area during the first half of the 1800's. Hiram Martin Chittenden described the Yanktonais from the traders' point of view:

They were on the whole the most dreaded by the traders of any of the Sioux tribes. They were

---

[35]Hiram Martin Chittenden, *The American Fur Trade of the Far West*, 2 Vols. (Stanford, CA: Academic Reprints, 1954), Vol. 1, p. 323-26; Paul Chrisler Phillips, *The Fur Trade*, 2 Vols. (Norman: University of Oklahoma Press, 1961), Vol. 2, pp. 412, 415, 419; Doane Robinson, pp. 141, 161; Keating, Vol. 1, pp. 445-46.

treacherous, stealthy, vindictive, and caused a great deal of trouble. It was a frequent pastime with them to fire from some secure hiding place upon boats passing along the river. Small parties were never safe in their country, while the loss of life and property at their hands during the period of the fur trade was such as to cause never-ending solicitude on the part of those who did business among them.[36]

Denig, a trader on the upper Missouri for over 20 years, probably explained the cause of at least a portion of this hostility when in 1855 he wrote:

Of late years the Yanktonais have become maliciously disposed toward the U.S. Government and traders in the country. They were not at the Laramie Treaty and have by some means become infected with the spirit of hostility and dissatisfaction spreading through the whole nation, originating in the sickness and famine brought about by the western emigration along the Platte Trail.[37]

Smallpox

The sickness which Denig mentioned very likely included a devastating smallpox epidemic which started in the summer of 1837. This outbreak killed about 15,000 Indians in the upper Missouri area and caused a considerable amount of Indian hostility towards whites. An American Fur Company steamboat carried the disease up the river where it broke out first among the Mandans. Estimates of the number of Indians killed during the epidemic vary, but the disastrous effects are clear. The Mandans were almost exterminated as a tribe: one

---

[36]Chittenden, Vol. 2, p. 864.

[37]Hurt, *Sioux Indians II*, p. 207.

source states that they were reduced "in a few weeks from about sixteen hundred to thirty-one souls," while another indicates that their "population fell in a few months from about 1,800 to some 125." The disease also spread to other tribes, including the Hidatsas, Arikaras, Sioux, Blackfeet, Assiniboins, Crees, Crows, Pawnees, and so on. One government report mentioned that "over sixty lodges of Yanktonais Dakota – perhaps four hundred persons – died by this disease about the same time."[38]

The Yanktonais were traditional enemies of the Chippewas while living in central Minnesota. After the Assiniboins broke away from the Yanktonais and later moved onto the northern plains, they were considered enemies as well. Although the Yanktonais raided the villages of the riverine Arikara, Mandan and Hidatsa and treated them as enemies, "there were many peaceful interludes which permitted cultural exchange and intermarriage." As an example of this, "Medicine-bear's band of Yanktonai contained many people descended from captured Nuptadi Mandan women, including Medicine-bear himself."[39]

Games and Pictographs

Recreation, music and storytelling played a part in the Yanktonai culture. One of the field games which the Yanktonais played was called la crosse. Pike described a game of "the cross" in which he watched a group of Sioux Indians compete against a group of *Puants* (Winnebagoes) and *Reynards* (Foxes):

---

[38]Elwyn Robinson, pp. 97-98; J.W. Powell, ed., *Seventeenth Annual Report of the Bureau of American Ethnology, 1895-96* (Washington: Government Printing Office, 1898), Part 1, pp. 274-75.

[39]Howard, "Middle Dakota," p. 7.

The ball is made of some hard substance and covered with leather, the cross sticks are round and net work, with handles of three feet long ... the goals are set up on the prairie at the distance of half a mile. The ball is thrown up in the middle, and each party strives to drive it to the opposite goal; and when either party gains the first rubber, which is driving it quick round the post, the ball is again taken to the centre, the ground changed, and the contest renewed; and this is continued until one side gains four times.

Pike said that the Indians bet on these games, "sometimes to the amount of some thousand dollars," and added that "it is an interesting sight to see two or three hundred naked savages contending on the plain" during the game.[40]

The Yanktonais also played field games known as shinny and hoop-and-pole, and the women played gambling games referred to as bowl dice and the hand game. Yanktonai musical instruments included "the single-head tambour drum, the large dance drum, and the tall water drum." Hide, deer-hoof and gourd rattles were used.[41]

The artistic work of the Yanktonais appeared in various forms. Both floral and geometric designs were used in quillwork and beadwork.[42] Tipis were sometimes decorated with pictographs. Winter counts, a series of pictographs depicting the important events of each year, served as a record of tribal and personal history.

A surviving Dakota tipi is located in the museum of the Oklahoma Historical Society at Oklahoma City. Covered with 125 scenes or pictographs, it was acquired at Fort Rice along the Missouri River in 1866 and is believed to have been obtained from "either a northern sub-band of the Teton Dakota, or the nearby Yanktonai Dakota." Both groups made

---

[40]Pike, p. 100.

[41]Howard, "Middle Dakota," pp. 5-6.

[42]*Ibid.*, p. 5.

similar tipis and drew pictographs on them when possible. Almost two-thirds of the scenes deal with some aspect of battle, while the remaining drawings depict animals, hunting, courtship and other aspects of tribal culture.[43]

Winter counts used similar drawings on hides and pieces of cloth to serve as an annual record. These "calendars" provided "a picture of a single outstanding event for each year."[44] Several winter counts, for example, indicate that a group of Arikaras under Chief Red Elk spent the winter of 1851-52 with a group of Upper Yanktonais, camping near the present town of Washburn, North Dakota.[45]

Religion and the Sun Dance

The religion of the Yanktonais, and of the Dakotas in general, was centered around the supreme being, "Wakan Tanka," which translates as "Great Mystery." Wakan Tanka included all the forces in the universe and was believed to be the creator of all things. A number of subordinate deities were also recognized, including Thunder, which was located to the west. When worshiping or invoking these deities, the Indians pointed a ceremonial pipe in each of the four directions, and toward the sky and earth as well.[46]

These Indians believed that after death the souls went to "Wanare Tebe, or the dwelling-place of the souls." Not everyone completed this journey, however, and Keating described the two possible alternatives. Those who failed to

---

[43]Sam Reynolds, "A Dakota Tipi", *North Dakota History*, 40-4 (Fall, 1973), pp. 20-29.

[44]James H. Howard, "Dakota Winter Counts as a Source of Plains History," *Anthropological Papers, Numbers 57-62*, Smithsonian Institution Bureau of American Ethnology, Bulletin 173 (Washington: Government Printing Office, 1960), No. 61, p. 339.

[45]Howard, "Middle Dakota," p. 7.

[46]Hassrick, pp. 205-208; Keating, Vol. 1, pp. 408-409; Curtis, pp. 60-61.

reach Wanare Tebe went "to the region of the evil spirit, where they are kept constantly chopping wood, carrying water, &c. being frequently flogged by their relentless master." Those who completed the long journey reached "the habitation of the Wahkan Tanka, or Great Spirit," where "their life is an easy and a blissful one, they hunt the buffalo, plant corn, &c."[47]

The Yanktonais used the scaffold method of burial for their dead, believing that the ghost of a person buried in the ground would come back to haunt the living. Soon after death, the body was dressed in fine clothing, and the face was painted red. The body was then wrapped securely in several skins and lashed to a scaffold consisting of a high platform supported by four poles. The dead were often placed on platforms in trees in the same manner. After decomposition, the body was sometimes buried in the ground.[48]

Yanktonai shamans, or medicine-men, were divided into classes according to their healing procedures and ceremonies, and these were named after the spirit-animals that provided them.[49]

Those who had been "blessed" by the bison were the tribal surgeons. The shamans with bear "power" were skilled in the use of herb medicines, while the Little-tree-dweller shamans specialized in the treatment of what today would be termed allergies.[50]

The Yanktonais observed a number of religious ceremonies, among which were the Mystery Dance, held annually to give medicine-men an opportunity to demonstrate

---

[47]Keating, Vol. 1, p. 410.

[48]Howard, "Middle Dakota," p. 6; David I. Bushnell, Jr., *Burials West of the Mississippi*, Smithsonian Institution Bureau of American Ethnology, Bulletin 83 (Washington: Government Printing Office, 1927), p. 28; Curtis, p. 140.

[49]Curtis, p. 140; Howard, "Middle Dakota," p. 6.

[50]Howard, "Middle Dakota," p. 6.

the strength of their medicines; the Buffalo Chant, a puberty ceremony for girls; and the Ghost Keeper rite, performed to show respect for someone who had died.[51] Other Yanktonai ceremonies included the Grass Dance, which involved a warrior society,[52] and the Bear Cult ceremony, in which a ceremonial bear hunt was performed.[53] Howard stated that the Sun Dance may have been the most important religious ceremony observed by these Indians,[54] and Keating described the circumstances under which Waneta decided to observe this rite:

> In the summer of 1822 he undertook a journey, from which, apprehending much danger on the part of the Chippewas, he made a vow to the Sun, that, if he returned safe, he would abstain from all food or drink for the space of four successive days and nights, and that he would distribute among his people all the property which he possessed, including all his lodges, horses, dogs, &c.

Waneta did not meet with misfortune on this trip, and after his return, "he celebrated the dance of the sun":

> This consisted in making three cuts through his skin, one on his breast, and one on each of his arms. The skin was cut in the manner of a loop, so as to permit a rope to pass between the flesh and the strip of skin which was thus divided from the body. The ropes being passed through, their ends were secured to a tall vertical pole, planted at about forty yards from his

---

[51]Curtis, pp. 99, 122, 140.

[52]James H. Howard, "Notes on the Dakota Grass Dance", *Southwestern Journal of Anthropology*, 7 (Spring, 1951; Reprint ed., Albuquerque: University of New Mexico Press), pp. 82-85.

[53]John C. Ewers, *Indian Life on the Upper Missouri* (Norman: University of Oklahoma Press, 1968), pp. 134-36.

[54]Howard, "Middle Dakota," p. 5.

lodge. He then began to dance round this pole, at the commencement of this fast, frequently swinging himself in the air, so as to be supported merely by the cords which were secured to the strips of skin separated from his arms and breast.[55]

Waneta kept up this dance, with few intermissions, until mid-morning of the fourth day "when the strip of skin from his breast gave way." After this he continued to dance until the strip of skin from his left arm broke apart at noon. His uncle then used a knife to cut the skin from his right arm, after which Waneta collapsed on the ground. "He was left exposed in that state to the sun until night, when his friends brought him some provisions."[56]

The tribal culture of the Yanktonais, including their religious ceremonies, illustrates their adaptation to the plains environment. When the American frontier was pushed westward into the Dakota area in the 1800's, the white men encountered Indians who derived their food, clothing, tools, utensils, weapons, and dwellings primarily from the buffalo. With horses, the Yanktonais were able to move easily and often on the prairies.

---

[55]Keating, Vol. 1, p. 449.
[56]*Ibid.*, pp. 449-50.

Chapter 5

Minnesota Sioux Uprising

Following the Louisiana Purchase in 1803, American contact with the Yanktonai and Hunkpatina Indians increased through both explorers and fur traders. The War of 1812 temporarily interrupted much of the American activity in the upper Missouri area, but in the early 1820's both government expeditions and fur trading parties were again traveling through this territory. In 1825 the United States government negotiated two treaties with the Yanktonais and other tribes, illustrating the extent of American interest in the region.

Two 1825 Treaties

During the summer of 1825, General Henry Atkinson and Major Benjamin O'Fallon met with a number of tribes along the Missouri River. They had been appointed to make peace treaties with these tribes after traders had experienced troubles with the Arikara and Blackfoot.[1] By establishing treaties of peace and friendship with these tribes, the United States also hoped to eliminate encroachment by British

---

[1]Hurt, *Sioux Indians II*, p. 172.

traders along the upper Missouri.[2] Atkinson and O'Fallon, accompanied by over 400 troups, negotiated a treaty with Teton, Yankton and Yanktonai bands at Fort Lookout along the Missouri River on June 22, and then traveled up the Missouri to the mouth of the Teton River where a similar treaty was signed by "Sioune and Ogallala" bands on July 5, 1825. The agreement at Fort Lookout did not include a list of the Yanktonais who signed, and it appears that these Indians were included among the Yankton and Teton signers. The Sioune band which signed later with the Ogallalas also included Yanktonais, since "Wah-e-ne-ta, the Rushing Man," was listed among the chiefs who signed on July 5.[3]

In these treaties, the Indians acknowledged the right of the United States to regulate all trade and intercourse with them, agreed to exert themselves to recover horses and other property stolen from Americans, and promised not to furnish guns to tribes that were hostile to the United States. In return, the United States promised to provide friendship and protection, and to furnish licensed traders in their territory.[4]

General William Clark and Lewis Cass, governor of Michigan Territory, also conducted negotiations with a number of Indian tribes in 1825. They hoped to make peace among the tribes and to end the conflicts which the Sioux had been having with the Chippewas, the Sacs and Foxes, and the Iowas. Clark and Cass therefore arranged for a large council to be held at Prairie du Chien on the Mississippi River. The Yanktonais were represented by "Wan-na-ta, he that charges on his enemies," when the resulting treaty was signed by numerous chiefs on August 19, 1825.[5]

The treaty at Prairie du Chien established specific territories and boundaries for each of the tribes involved: Sioux,

---

[2]Anderson, p. 14.

[3]Kappler, pp. 227-32;   Doane Robinson, pp. 146, 150-53.

[4]Kappler, pp. 227-31.

[5]*Ibid.*, p. 254;   Doane Robinson, pp. 143-46.

Chippewa, Sac and Fox, Menominee, Iowa, Winnebago, Ottawa and Potawatomi. Each tribe gave up any claim to land designated as the territory of another tribe, and it was agreed "that no tribe shall hunt within the acknowledged limits of any other without their assent." The treaty stated that it was "the sole object of this arrangement to perpetuate a peace" among the tribes.[6] It has been observed, however, that "the United States wanted those divisions to facilitate land cessions," and that soon afterwards government agents began acquiring these lands, each of which could then be claimed by only one tribe.[7]

It is important to note that a chief did not have the authority to sign a treaty on behalf of his tribe without consulting with tribal members first. A council of influential members of the tribe was called to consider the issue and to determine the course of action to be followed. Any treaty signed by a chief without following this procedure had little effect.

Treaties in 1851 and 1858

After 1825, the Yanktonais do not appear to have been involved in another treaty with the United States for 40 years. They were not invited to the proceedings of the 1851 Fort Laramie Treaty which opened the central plains for transportation routes through Kansas and Nebraska, even though the western Sioux were asked to attend. According to one source, "The Yanktonais were omitted because their country was between the headwaters of the Minnesota River in eastern South Dakota and the Missouri – an area far removed from

---

[6]Kappler, pp. 250-53.

[7]Ray Allen Billington, *Westward Expansion: A History of the American Frontier*, 4th ed. (New York: Macmillan Publishing Co., 1974), p. 286.

Under treaties signed in 1851, the Santee Sioux ceded much of their tribal homeland in Minnesota to the United States government. Eleven years later animosity over the loss of their lands and other grievances led to the Minnesota Uprising. This painting by Francis D. Millet of the 1851 treaty signed at Traverse des Sioux is in the Minnesota Capitol in St. Paul, MN.

Photo from Minnesota
Historical Society

64

the overland route to the Pacific coast which the treaty aimed to safeguard."[8]

The Yanktonais were also omitted from the 1851 treaty in which the Santee Sioux ceded much of their Minnesota homeland to the United States in return for $3 million in annuities payable over 50 years. The four Santee tribes were left with a reservation 150 miles long and 20 miles wide along the Minnesota River.[9] The Yanktonais were angered by this cession, asserting that they also had a claim to these lands.[10]

In an 1858 treaty the Santees sold the portion of their reservation north of the Minnesota River to the government, cutting the size of their reservation in half.[11] Yanktonais sometimes showed up for the annual distribution of annuities on the Minnesota reservation, hoping to receive a share.[12] The Yanktons also signed a treaty with the United States in 1858, relinquishing all of their lands except for a 400,000 acre reservation in return for $1.6 million in annuities to be paid over 50 years. The Yanktonais, along with the Tetons and some of the Yanktons, opposed this treaty and claimed rights to the ceded lands.[13]

In 1858 and 1859 unsuccessful efforts were made by the government to meet with the Yanktonais. "These efforts," according to one historian, "were motivated in part by the trouble caused by the Yanktonais, who, after their Mississippi Sioux cousins began to receive annuities under the 1851 treaties, complained . . . that they had improperly been left out of the 1851 treaties."[14]

---

[8]Indian Claims Commission, *Sioux Indians IV* (New York: Garland Publishing, 1974), p. 171.

[9]Charles M. Oehler, *The Great Sioux Uprising* (New York: Oxford University Press, 1959), p. 12.

[10]Anderson, p. 12.

[11]Oehler, p. 12.

[12]Doane Robinson, pp. 241, 266.

[13]*Ibid.*, pp. 248-49.

[14]Anderson, pp. 25-26.

In the late 1850's, a renegade band of Santees led by Inkpaduta (or Scarlet Point) apparently moved west to the prairies and associated with the Yanktonais. Inkpaduta, a Wahpekute chief, was considered an outlaw by both Santees and whites. His band was said to have killed 18 Wahpekute warriors while they were asleep in a hunting camp in 1849, and in 1857 they killed 42 white settlers in two neighboring settlements near Spirit Lake, Iowa. After the "Spirit Lake Massacre," Inkpaduta supposedly moved west to the Yanktonai area where he successfully evaded both infantry detachments and other Santees who sought to apprehend him.[15]

When Dakota Territory was established in 1861, the Yanktonais and Hunkpatinas occupied much of the area east of the Missouri River. Events which followed the Minnesota Uprising of 1862 rapidly changed this, however.

---

[15]Despite the attention Inkpaduta has received in regional history, he remains an enigma. Doane Robinson, a South Dakota historian, linked Inkpaduta to almost every significant incident of Sioux hostility in the early 1860's, placing him in Minnesota for the 1862 uprising, in eastern Dakota Territory in 1863 for the three battles with Sibley's troops and the battle at Whitestone Hill with Sully's men, and west of the Missouri in 1864 for the battle at Killdeer Mountain and the skirmishes in the Badlands. Robinson also charged Inkpaduta with responsibility for well known individual murders, including those of a man named Jacobson near Yankton, SD, and the Wiseman family in Nebraska.

Robinson said that Inkpaduta's "ubiquity was amazing," but also felt it necessary to mention the possibility that he may have been used as a scapegoat by other Indians who "desire to relieve themselves of responsibility" for the hostilities. Robinson listed Joseph LaFrambois and John B. Renville among his sources, and dated his conversations with them around 1900, almost 40 years after these events occurred. Renville and LaFrambois obviously had acquired much of their information from other people since they were not witnesses to many of these events.

The use of Inkpaduta as a scapegoat seems quite probable in many cases. Other sources have carried Inkpaduta's career through to the battle of Little Big Horn in 1876, and some have even claimed that Custer was killed by one of Inkpaduta's sons.

Doane Robinson, pp. 342-47; Daniel Buck, *Indian Outbreaks* (Minneapolis: Ross & Haines, 1965), pp. 32-38; Kenneth Carley, *The Sioux Uprising of 1862* (St. Paul: Minnesota Historical Society, 1976), p. 5; Peggy Larson, "Inkpaduta – Renegade Sioux" (Unpublished Master's thesis, Mankato State College, Mankato, MN, 1969), pp. 70, 87-89.

Minnesota Uprising of 1862

A number of grievances among the Santees, some of them dating back to the 1851 treaty, came to a head in 1862. Under the 1851 and 1858 treaties, the Santees had sold much of their land to the U.S. Government. About 6,600 Santee Sioux were living in groups along the Minnesota River in 1862 (the Sisseton and Wahpeton bands on the upper part of the reservation, and the Mdewakanton and Wahpekute along the lower portion).[16] Many Santees resented the loss of their lands through treaties.

The Santees had other grievances in addition to the loss of their lands. Subsidies were given to Indians who would farm on the reservation, but nine-tenths of the Santees refused to take up agriculture and resented this special treatment which farmer Indians received. Each year white traders defrauded the Indians out of much of their annuity money. The Indian agents were believed to be in collusion with the crooked traders. In 1862, the annuities arrived late and then were not distributed immediately when a portion of them did arrive. This angered the Santees even further.[17]

An incident on August 17, 1862, triggered the Indian uprising in Minnesota. Four young Wahpetons returning from an unsuccessful hunting trip murdered five settlers in Meeker County, Minnesota. News of this spread rapidly through the reservation.[18] Two of the more hostile chiefs called for a council early the next morning, and Little Crow[19]

---

[16]Robert Huhn Jones, *The Civil War in the Northwest: Nebraska, Wisconsin, Iowa, Minnesota, and the Dakotas* (Norman: University of Oklahoma Press, 1960), p. 18.

[17]Oehler, pp. 24-25.

[18]*Ibid.*, pp. 3-9.

[19]Little Crow, a Mdewakanton chief, was the best known leader on the lower portion of the reservation. He had played a significant part in the treaties of 1851 and 1858 and had become a farmer Indian when the Santees moved onto the reservation. Little Crow's prestige and authority prompted his selection as leader of the uprising. Oehler, pp. 17-21, 30.

was chosen to lead an uprising to kill and drive out the whites. Shakopee, Red Middle Voice and Medicine Bottle were also among the hostiles. In the days that followed, Santees raided settlements and cabins, massacred whites, and unsuccessfully attacked both Fort Ridgely and New Ulm. One-third of New Ulm was destroyed as a result of the attacks.

Forty thousand settlers fled in response to the Indian attacks, and the white casualties were later estimated to be at least 800. But it soon became apparent to the hostiles that they were not going to be able to drive out the whites permanently. Colonel Henry Hastings Sibley arrived at Fort Ridgely with 1,500 troops ten days after the uprising began. The hostile Indians were unable to defeat the soldiers in battles at Birch Coulee and Wood Lake. When Sibley reached the reservation, he demanded that the Indians surrender.[20]

Sibley set up a military tribunal which conducted questionable trials for nearly 400 of the Indians who either surrendered or were captured.[21] Three hundred and six were sentenced to hang, but President Abraham Lincoln changed this list and only 38 were hanged in December. Indian prisoners who were not hanged spent three years at a camp in Iowa before they were released. The other Santees from the reservation who surrendered were sent to Crow Creek along the Missouri River in Dakota Territory. Not all of the Santees had been hostile during the uprising. Bands of Sissetons and Wahpetons on the upper part of the reservation did not take part in the massacres.[22]

Many of the hostile Santees, and some who had not been hostile but feared reprisals if they remained on the reservation, fled to Dakota Territory and Canada after the battle at

---

[20]Oehler, pp. xiii-xvi.

[21]Richard L. Mackie, "The Trial and Execution of Sioux Indian Prisoners after the Minnesota Uprising of 1862" (Unpublished Master's thesis, University of Wisconsin-Eau Claire, 1972), pp. 8-16.

[22]Oehler, pp. 208-22, 225, 239-40.

Little Crow, Santee Sioux Chief

Photo from Smithsonian Institution

Wood Lake. Little Crow and many other hostiles spent the winter in the area around Devils Lake in Dakota Territory.[23]

---

[23]Oehler, pp. 224-25.

Chapter 6

Soldiers Enter Dakota Territory

During the winter of 1862-63, General John Pope, commander of the Department of the Northwest, made plans to send troops to Dakota Territory the following summer. Pope had been in command of the Union armies in Virginia when they were defeated at the Second Battle of Bull Run in August, 1862. Soon afterward he was sent west to take charge of the Department of the Northwest which had been created to protect settlements in Wisconsin, Iowa, Minnesota, and the Territories of Dakota and Nebraska.[1]

Settlers on the frontier were afraid of further Indian hostilities following the 1862 Minnesota Uprising. Some of the hostile Santee Sioux had fled west from Minnesota onto the Dakota prairies. In addition, reports and rumors indicated unrest among the Sioux who traditionally lived in Dakota Territory, including the Yanktonais and even the Tetons. Public pressure from newspapers, politicians, and the general population demanded that the Army take action to protect the frontier settlements.

---

[1]Geraldine Bean, "General Alfred Sully and the Northwest Indian Expedition," *North Dakota History*, 33-3 (Summer, 1966), p. 244.

The Campaign Plan

Under General Pope's plan, a large military force led by General Sibley (he had been promoted to brigadier general following the Minnesota battles the previous fall) would leave Fort Ridgely in Minnesota and travel in a northwesterly direction into Dakota Territory. Sibley's force would engage the Indians near Devils Lake and drive them southwest toward the Missouri River. General John Cook, with another military force, would start from Sioux City, Iowa, and follow the Missouri River north until he was in position to cut off the retreat of the Indians encountered by Sibley. With this two-pronged campaign, the two armies would be able to crush the Indians between them.[2]

Before the 1863 expeditions could get under way, however, the War Department decided to replace General Cook. Pope wanted to put one of his former staff members in charge of the column going up the Missouri, but he was overruled and notified that General Alfred Sully was being sent west to assume this command, a decision Pope appears to have resented.[3]

Sully, a career army officer, had graduated from West Point in 1841 and spent much of the next 20 years on the frontier in Indian campaigns. "He served against the Seminoles in Florida in 1841 and 1842, against the Rogue River Indians in California and Oregon in the late 1840s and early 1850s, against the Sioux in the Northwest in the mid-1850s, and against the southern Cheyenne in 1860. Either in his capacity as a soldier or as a treaty negotiator, he had dealings with most of the plains tribes – the Santee-Sioux, Winnebagoes, Chippewas, Teton-Sioux, Omahas, Poncas, Pawnees, Cheyennes, Rees, Mandans, Gros Ventres, and

---

[2]Jones, p. 61; Bean, pp. 245-46.

[3]Langdon Sully, *No Tears for the General: The Life of Alfred Sully, 1821-1879* (Palo Alto, CA: American West Publishing Co., 1974), p. 166.

General Alfred Sully

Photo from State Historical Society of North Dakota

Crows." He had also distinguished himself while with the Union Army in 1862 by keeping the defeat at the Second Battle of Bull Run from turning into a rout.[4]

Iowa and Nebraska Soldiers

Sully's troops for the expedition into Dakota Territory consisted primarily of volunteers from two neighboring areas: the state of Iowa and Nebraska Territory. These men were not professional soldiers. Most were settlers who had moved to the western frontier, found the land and life style to their liking, and decided to make their homes. When finally assembled, Sully's force numbered roughly 2,000 men.[5]

Many of the volunteers who joined the 6th Iowa Cavalry had expected to be sent east to fight Confederate troops in the Civil War.[6] In January, 1863, one soldier wrote to friends that "the quicker we get to dixie . . . the better it will be for our name as a loyal regiment." Two months later, however, the Iowa volunteers learned that they would be heading west and north to fight Indians instead of east to fight Southerners. Their destination would be Dakota Territory.[7]

Diaries, journals and letters reveal aspects of the day to day life of the soldiers. As the Iowa troops marched toward the Dakotas that spring, Pvt. Milton Spencer wrote that settlers' chickens had become a favorite food among the soldiers. He noted that "Chickens have a great dread of

---

[4]Bean, p. 247.

[5]George W. Kingsbury, *History of Dakota Territory* (Chicago: S.J. Clarke Publishing Co., 1915), Vol. 1, p. 288.

[6]J.H. Drips, *Three Years Among the Indians in Dakota* (New York: Sol Lewis, 1974), p. 2; Frank Myers, *Soldiering in Dakota, Among the Indians* (Freeport, NY: Books for Libraries Press, 1971), p. 3.

[7]Carol G. Goodwin, "The Letters of Private Milton Spencer, 1862-1865: A Soldier's View of Military Life on the Northern Plains," *North Dakota History*, 37-4 (Fall, 1970), p. 237.

soldiers and will hide as soon as they get sight of a blue jacket or brass buttons." The soldiers often bought chickens from settlers along their route and occasionally even resorted to confiscating the farmers' fowl. Later Spencer added, "I guess the 6th Iowa will long be remembered along this road for their terrible charges against the chickens."

Spencer, with the tongue-in-cheek view of a young soldier, at one point observed that the weather was good, "except being verry windy – blowing so much dust in my eyes that I could not tell whether the girls along the road were handsome or homely."[8]

The 2nd Nebraska Cavalry, unlike its 6th Iowa Cavalry counterpart, was recruited primarily to provide protection from Indian hostilities on the frontier. They were to be the home protection force for Nebraska Territory while many other Nebraska men were engaged in the Civil War.[9] While the 6th Iowa soldiers had signed up for three years of military service, the 2nd Nebraska men had volunteered for a nine month tour of duty.

Delays Along the Way

The expedition of Iowa and Nebraska soldiers did not get started into Dakota Territory as early as had been planned, partly because of a delay in the arrival of the 2nd Nebraska Cavalry.[10] Ole Johnson, an enlisted man in the 6th Iowa Cavalry who had emigrated from Norway, made the following entry in his diary at Camp Cook on May 5th: "In the knight the New Braskey cavilry com hear to Camp Kook."[11]

---

[8]Goodwin, p. 239.

[9]Richard D. Rowen, ed., "The Second Nebraska's Campaign Against the Sioux," *Nebraska History*, 44-1 (March, 1963), pp. 3-4.

[10]Bean, p. 246.

[11]"Record of Ole Johnson of Co. D, 6th Iowa Cavalry" (Archives, State Historical Society of North Dakota, Bismarck).

The 6th Iowa
Cavalry shown
in camp on the
march north to
Dakota Ter-
ritory in the
Spring of 1863.

*Photo from State
Historical Society
of North Dakota*

Another factor in the expedition not getting started as early as General Pope had planned was that General Sully did not assume command until June 1. Then, once underway, Sully's army was delayed even more by exceptionally low water on the Missouri River. The steamboats carrying Sully's supplies up the river had to move slowly and often got hung up on sandbars.[12]

As the army marched through southern Dakota Territory in early June, Pvt. Spencer described the countryside for his father in a letter, but commented that this description would probably "be like the country, verry dry." The shortages of good water and grass for the horses were major concerns for the soldiers. Spencer added that:

> The grass has now disappeared on the prairie and is only to be found along the banks of the creeks. I say disappeared, but not entirely for the prairie is covered with a short brown substance which I suppose is called grass but it dont look much like it. It looks as though it was a dozen years old and had been without rain or dew all its life.[13]

The expedition made an impressive effort to do the majority of its marching early in the day, before the hottest part of the afternoon. Corporal Henry Pierce, a member of the 2nd Nebraska Cavalry, described this practice in the June 24 entry in his diary: "At 2 o'clock this morning the reveillee sounded. In a few minutes all was astir, breakfast got & ate, horses fed, saddled & packed, & at 4 o'clock the column was again in motion . . . ."[14]

Soldiers' meals were typically determined by the type of food available. In a letter, one soldier wrote that he was about to "go and boil some rice, fry some bacon, make some coffee,

---

[12]Kingsbury, p. 289.

[13]Goodwin, pp. 242-43.

[14]Rowen, p. 25.

and with a hard cracker or two make out my supper." The expedition's food supply included cattle which were slaughtered from time to time. When possible, the soldiers hunted wild game such as antelope, buffalo, and rabbit, and were encouraged to gather wild berries. The basic diet consisted primarily of "coffee, tea, hominy, rice, beans, sugar, molasses and vinegar."[15]

In early July, Cpl. Pierce wrote of having "traveled all day over a desolated country. No wood, no water, no grass except in ravines." Pierce concluded that the dry, sparse terrain even affected the prairie animals, adding, ". . . still no game except now & then a poor half starved rabbit, tugging along with a haver sack hanging to his neck."[16]

Sibley's Skirmishes

While Sully's troops were moving slowly up the Missouri River, General Sibley's expedition entered Dakota Territory in late June and headed towards Devils Lake. The Indians, however, knew about the approach of Sibley's army and had left that area. Sibley's troops found only Wowinapa, the son of Little Crow, who reported that his father had been killed earlier in Minnesota. Little Crow and his son had returned to western Minnesota in June to steal horses. On July 3, the chief was killed by settlers near Hutchinson. After his father's death, Wowinapa returned to the Devils Lake area on foot and was captured by Sibley's soldiers.[17]

Sibley's army then headed toward the Missouri River and made contact with a large body of Indians. The soldiers fought minor battles with these Indians at Big Mound, Dead Buffalo Lake and Stony Lake before the Indians crossed to

---

[15]Goodwin, p. 245; Rowen, p. 29.

[16]Rowen, p. 31.

[17]Oehler, pp. 229-32.

Officers of the 2nd Nebraska Cavalry
Seated (left to right): Col. Robert W. Furnas, Lt. Col. William F. Sapp, Surgeon Aurelius Bowen, Major George Armstrong. Standing: Major John Taffe, Major John W. Pearman, Adjutant Henry M. Atkinson.

Photo from State Historical Society of North Dakota

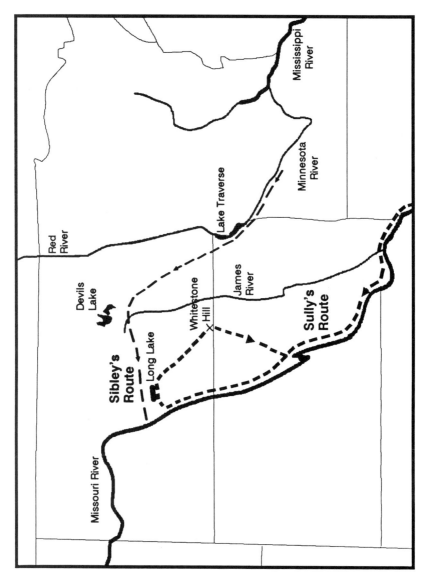

1863 Campaign

Two military expeditions entered Dakota Territory during the summer of 1863. One column of soldiers was led by General Henry H. Sibley and originated from Minnesota. The other expedition, commanded by General Alfred Sully, followed the Missouri River north from Iowa. Sully's campaign culminated in the Battle at Whitestone Hill.

the west side of the Missouri. Sibley waited for Sully's column along the river for two days and then started back to Minnesota on August 1.[18]

The delay of Sully's expedition along the Missouri drew strong criticism from General Pope. In an August 5 letter to Sully, Pope stressed the need to move north rapidly to meet Sibley's force: "Such a failure as you anticipate must not happen, as it will be impossible for you to explain it satisfactorily." In an August 20 letter to Henry W. Halleck, General-in-Chief of the Union Armies, Pope wrote: "General Sully has not made the progress which was expected of him, and which it was in his power to have made ...."[19]

The possibility of a battle with Indians was clearly on the minds of Sully's troops. In early August, a Nebraska soldier wrote that "the expiration of the time of service of the 2nd Neb is nearly to a close. Men appear to be all anxious to see & have a brush with the indians before their discharge." A week later one of the Iowa soldiers mentioned that "Gen. Sully had promised to show us some Indians to fight before we got back ...."[20]

In addition to low water on the Missouri which delayed the arrival of supplies, Sully's expedition was also occasionally hampered by the weather. Ole Johnson, the Iowa soldier who had emigrated from Norway, described an August 19th hailstorm as "raining harder den I have ever seen et and haild big as hen eggs raind and haild about 1 our."[21] Sgt. J.H. Drips, also a member of the 6th Iowa Cavalry, left another vivid account of this hailstorm:

---

[18]Jones, pp. 63-66.

[19]U.S. Department of War, *The War of The Rebellion: A Compilation of the Official Records of the Union and Confederate Armies*, Series I, Vol. XXII, Part II – Correspondence, (Washington: Government Printing Office, 1888), pp. 434, 464. (Hereafter referred to as *Correspondence*).

[20]Rowen, p. 37; Drips, p. 36.

[21]Johnson diary.

After raining about an hour it commenced to hail and oh, such hail! This continued for about an hour, the stones flying as thick as hail generally falls and the size of the stones was about, on an average, the size of a pigeon's egg; some of them a good deal larger, even to the size of a hen's egg. I tell you, when they came down on a poor soldier's pate it was unpleasant in the extreme.[22]

As the expedition moved north along the Missouri River, anti-Indian sentiment increased among Sully's troops. Contributing to this was the news that in July the five children of Pvt. Henson Wiseman, one of the 2nd Nebraska soldiers, had been killed in their home by Sioux Indians.[23] Another Nebraska volunteer expressed the anger of the troops:

Where is the home protection forces that was raised with such confidence & assurance of remaining to protect its own soil. They have gone from their homes, their wives & the babes that are dearest to their life, & the Indians have fallen in our rear commenced their savage & brutal massacres.[24]

Searching for Indians

Although unable to meet up with Sibley, Sully decided to make a brief swing of his own east of the Missouri River. On August 21, he broke away from the Missouri at the mouth of the Little Cheyenne River and traveled northeast toward Devils Lake. He planned a brief swing because he only had rations for 23 days. On August 26, his scouting party brought

---

[22]Drips, p. 39.

[23]Doane Robinson, p. 329.

[24]Rowen, p. 38.

Two soldiers in the 6th Iowa Cavalry found time to inscribe their names on a sandstone rock while Sully's expedition was in the Long Lake area. August Brandes was 20 years old, lived in McGregor, Iowa, and was of German ancestry. Griffin Gager, age 33, was from Plymouth Rock, Iowa, and was born in Canada. This stone is displayed in the North Dakota Heritage Center museum in Bismarck.

Photo from State Historical Society of North Dakota

83

in two Indian women and some children who said that Sibley had fought Indians near Long Lake.[25]

After heading east away from the Missouri, the expedition also began to encounter large herds of buffalo. While scouting parties were out searching for Indians, some of the other soldiers decided to try their hands at buffalo hunting. On August 25, Col. Robert Furnas of the 2nd Nebraska Cavalry wrote about having seen numerous buffalo, adding that the "command halted and a great many of the boys went in pursuit and were quite successful one horse was shot and a matter of surprise that many more were not as most of them who went out were inexperienced." The following day Furnas described a similar situation:

> During the day thousands of Buffalo were seen in every direction A great many were killed Lt. Stewart Co. E killed his horse by an accidental shot. At night the Genl issued an order forbidding any more hunting until on the return . . . ."[26]

Sully's force reached the outlet of Long Lake on August 28, found signs of large numbers of Indians, and found an old crippled Indian who said that Sibley had fought the Indians some weeks earlier. The Indian said that a few days after Sibley had left the Missouri the Indians had recrossed the river, that they had discovered a Mackinaw boat going down the river and had killed the 24 people on board before sinking it, and that a large portion of the Indians had headed toward Long Lake.[27]

---

[25]*U.S. Department of War, The War of The Rebellion: A Compilation of the Official Records of the Union and Confederate Armies*, Series I, Vol. XXII, Part I – Official Records, (Washington: Government Printing Office, 1888), p. 556. (Hereafter referred to as *Official Records*).

[26]Rowen, p. 21.

[27]*Official Records*, p. 556.

Sully's guides were familiar with the area of Dakota Territory into which they were heading and told him:

"... always at this season of the year the Indians camped on the Coteau, near the tributaries of the James, where the numerous lakes or springs kept the grass fresh; here the buffalo were plenty, and the lakes and streams full of fish; and that here they prepared their meat for the winter, moving to the Missouri, where the fuel was plenty, to winter."[28]

In this report Sully is referring to the Missouri Coteau, or Coteau de Missouri, a range of glacial moraines 5 to 20 miles wide and 300 to 400 feet high. In the Whitestone Hill area the coteau lies basically in a north-south direction with the land both east and west of the coteau being relatively flat. The uneven terrain of the coteau includes small hills, ravines, and many small lakes. The James River is about 30 miles east of Whitestone Hill and the Missouri River is about 85 miles to the west.[29]

On the basis of the information provided by his guides, Sully changed his course and headed southeast. In his report Sully described the area they traveled through:

... after a march of above 90 miles through a country with no wood whatever, but with good grass and plenty of lakes of the most abominable water, on the 3d of September we reached a lake, where, on the plains near by, were the remains of a very large number of buffaloes killed, some quite recently. Here I encamped to wait the reports of the commands I had out

[28]*Official Records*, p. 557.

[29]Frederick B. Loomis, *Physiography of the United States* (Garden City, NY: Doubleday, Doran & Co., 1937), p. 207; Nevin M. Fenneman, *Physiography of Western United States* (New York and London: McGraw-Hill Book Co., 1931), pp. 73-75.

during the march, who every day discovered fresh signs of Indians, their lodge trails spread over the country, but all moving toward a point known to be a favorite haunt of the Indians.[30]

Cpl. Pierce described the scene as the soldiers traveled on September 2: "At six o'clock our little army was again in motion. As it moves & meanders around the hills through ravines & over hilltops, it presents a somewhat grand appearance." During the march on Thursday, September 3, Col. Furnas noted having "passed 15 fresh Buffalo carcasses within sight of each other."[31] The soldiers knew there were Indians nearby.

---

[30]*Official Records*, p. 557.

[31] Rowen, pp. 46, 23.

Chapter 7

The Battle at Whitestone Hill

S couting parties were sent out daily to search for Indians as Sully's column headed toward the Missouri Coteau. These detachments of soldiers traveled in advance of or off to the side of the main column, moving faster and covering more territory and then returning to where the command had camped for the night to submit their reports. Such scouting missions had found evidence of Sibley's arrival and subsequent departure along the Missouri River, had encountered and brought in a few Indians, and had found lodge pole trails and other recent signs indicating the movement of large numbers of Indians toward the coteau.

Major House's Scouting Party

Early in the morning on September 3, a scouting party led by Major Albert E. House and consisting of four companies of the 6th Iowa Cavalry (about 300 men) left Sully's camp. Sully had instructed House to keep five miles ahead of the main command as they traveled during the day.[1] A mixed-

---

[1]*Official Records*, p. 557.

blood named Frank LaFrambois and an Indian known as Crazy Dog[2] served as guides for the scouting party. House traveled in a southerly direction, stopping to allow the horses to graze for 10 minutes of each hour. LaFrambois kept about five miles ahead of the scouting party and Crazy Dog traveled halfway between LaFrambois and the troops.[3] The area was hilly.

LaFrambois bore off much to the left of the general direction of march and in the afternoon discovered what he believed to be a small encampment of Indians, about 20 lodges.[4] He then returned to notify Major House who was resting his troops about two miles from the Indian encampment.[5]

House ordered his troops to load their weapons and the scouting party rode toward the Indian camp at a gallop. The troops were cautioned to keep in the valleys so they would not be seen by the Indians. E.A. Richards, an enlisted man in Company F of the 6th Iowa Cavalry, described the ride:

> Blankets got loose from the saddles and lariat ropes got loose and strung along on the ground, much to our annoyance. We were ordered to cut them loose and go as freely as possible, as we did not know where Gen. Sully and his command were and we might be com-

---

[2]Frank Meyers referred to this Indian as "Crazy Dog" while F.E. Caldwell used the name "Fool Dog." Amos Cherry of the 6th Iowa Cavalry had written favorably about Crazy Dog in a letter in May, 1863. According to Cherry, Crazy Dog was a member of the Fool Band of Yanktonais led by Bone Necklace. Cherry credited Crazy Dog with having rescued a young white girl from the Santees by trading his own horse for her freedom. Benjamin F. Shambaugh, ed., "Iowa Troops in the Sully Campaigns," *The Iowa Journal of History and Politics*, Vol. XX (1922), pp. 414-15.

[3]*Official Records*, p. 564; Drips, p. 53.

[4]*Official Records*, p. 567; Drips, p. 53.

[5]Distances used in the soldiers' accounts often conflict with one another. This was probably due to the difficulty of judging distance in the uneven terrain and to the fact that the soldiers were most likely preoccupied with other thoughts while they traveled. The distance between two points also probably depended on whether the troops were able to maintain the most direct route.

pelled to fight a fearful battle alone with our small army of about 300 men.[6]

Indians Camped at Whitestone Hill

The Indians were "camped on a little lake surrounded by hills which were covered with white stones."[7] When the scouting party neared the encampment, they discovered that it was much larger than expected. Two officers, sent forward for a closer look, reported that there were 400 lodges. Other estimates of the size of the camp vary between 300 and 600 lodges.[8] Figures concerning the number of Indians at the camp also vary, but the estimate of about 3,500 Indians, about 1,000 of whom were warriors, appears to be the most accurate.[9]

House dispatched LaFrambois and two soldiers to inform Sully of the situation and request reinforcements. While LaFrambois was riding for help,[10] the troops confronted the Indians who had discovered the scouting party as it approached the camp. House sent two companies to the left of

---

[6]Drips, p. 54.

[7]*Ibid.*

[8]*Official Records*, p. 559, 564, 566.

[9]Doane Robinson, p. 327.

[10]Sully, in his report, stated that LaFrambois was then surrounded by about 200 Indians who told him that "'they had fought General Sibley, and they could not see why the whites wanted to come and fight them, unless they were tired of living and wanted to die.' Mr. LaFrambois succeeded in getting away from them after some difficulty, and ran his horse a distance of more than 10 miles to give me information, Major House, with his command, still remaining there."

LaFrambois did reach Sully with the information about the scouting party, but this report of his encounter with the 200 Indians seems to be open to question. Major House's report does not mention the guide being stopped by Indians. Nor does E.A. Richards include this in his description of the guide's departure: "I can see him yet as he dashed away to the rear so as not to give the Indians any clue to his mission." If the Indians actually were hostile and had surrounded the guide, it is doubtful that LaFrambois could have gotten away.

Major Albert House

Photo from State Historical Society of North Dakota

the encampment to determine more closely the Indians' strength and position in the uneven terrain. After these companies had returned, he sent another company to the right of the camp, again to gain more information about the Indian defenses.[11]

When the Indians first saw the troops, "the young warriors rushed to the little lake and taking up some of the blue clay they daubed it over their bodies, marking themselves hideously, as they did not have time to get the regular war paint," according to Richards. He said that the young warriors wanted to fight the troops immediately but the older braves insisted that they wait until sundown.[12]

The confrontation between the scouting party and the Indian encampment must have lasted for about three hours. During this time some Indian chiefs approached the troops with a flag of truce and attempted to negotiate. "They offered to surrender some of their chiefs," but House said that since he "did not know who was entitled to speak by authority, he demanded the surrender of all. This they refused to do...."[13]

House's scouting party stalled for time while waiting for Sully to arrive with the main command. The soldiers stood in front of their horses with their guns ready and shifted their position occasionally to distract the Indians. They had "in-

---

[11]*Official Records*, p. 564.

[12]Drips, pp. 54-55.

[13]*Official Records*, p. 564.

structions not to fire under any circumstances," but to hold the Indians "in check till the rest of the command arrived."[14]

LaFrambois reached the main camp in the late afternoon. The bugle was sounded and the troops quickly brought in their grazing horses, saddled up, and formed in line. Sully left a small portion of the command at the camp and then headed for the Indian encampment at a gallop "with the Second Nebraska on the right, the Sixth Iowa on the left, one company of the Seventh Iowa and the battery in the center."[15]

The ride took about an hour. Pvt. Spencer conveyed the sense of urgency the soldiers felt as they rode rapidly toward the Indian camp: "Our horses did not walk much; several stumbled and fell, throwing their riders headlong."[16]

The sun was setting as Sully's force approached the Indian camp from the west. They were less than a mile away when the Indians saw them and prepared to make a hasty departure.

> Then the squaws and old men began taking down the teepes and loading the ponies with tent poles on either side with a strap over the back and the poles twelve to fifteen feet in length dragging on the ground. The squaws attended to this part. The pappooses were put in baskets and strapped on the poles which run from the ponies back to the ground. The wolf dogs were fixed up the same as the ponies were, only the packs were smaller. The young warriors were now fully aware of the danger and undertook to retreat to the James river, east a few miles.[17]

The Indians abandoned much of their equipment as they retreated.[18]

---

[14]Drips, p. 54-55.

[15]*Official Records*, p. 558.

[16]Goodwin, p. 250.

[17]Drips, pp. 55-56.

[18]*Official Records*, pp. 564-65.

When Sully saw the Indians departing, he told Colonel Furnas to push his 2nd Nebraska troops forward as fast as possible and to assist Major House's battalion in keeping the Indians surrounded. Furnas reached the scouting party and told House to pursue the left flank (north side) of the fleeing Indians while he went after the Indians on the right flank (south side).[19]

As the 2nd Nebraska Cavalry disappeared over the hills in a cloud of dust, Sully ordered Colonel Wilson to take the north side of the camp with part of the 6th Iowa Cavalry. Sully with some cavalry and the battery, went though the center of the Indian camp where he found a chief named Little Soldier with a few of his people. He placed these Indians under guard. Soon after that Sully came to "the notorious chief Big-head, and some of his men." This group of over 120 Indians surrendered. Members of "Medicine Bear's Band" were among the Indians who surrendered to Sully.[20]

One of the soldiers noted that they found the Indian camp "deserted by everything except a few dogs and squaws." He added that the departing Indians:

> ... had packed their dogs and ponys with a little dried meat and a small part of their household goods and were evidently bent on making their escape, but our scouting party had come upon them so suddenly that they seemed to think it best to wait for the night.[21]

By this time the different military commands appear to have been acting independently of each other. The various cavalry forces were spread out while trying to round up the Indians. Communications were understandably poor and no one appears to have been coordinating the efforts of the different battalions.

---

[19]*Official Records*, p. 566.

[20]*Official Records*, p. 558; Rowen, p. 24.

[21]Goodwin, p. 251.

The Indians scattered as they fled east attempting to escape. But as the troops gained on them, a large group of Indians gathered in a ravine about one half mile from the Indian camp.[22] This is where the battle took place.

When Colonel Furnas, with the 2nd Nebraska, came upon the Indians in the ravine, he formed his troops in a battle line. Furnas had then intended to wait for further orders from Sully, but changed his mind, as he explained:

> As it was then nearly dark, I felt that time was precious, and if anything was to be done that night it must be done speedily, and made up my mind to attack the enemy immediately.[23]

Furnas positioned his men in two lines which formed an obtuse angle and moved them forward.

> When within 400 yards, I ordered my men to dismount, and after advancing 100 yards nearer, ordered the Second Battalion to open the battle by a volley from their Enfields, which they did with precision and effect, creating quite a confusion in the enemy's ranks.[24]

Major House, with the Third Battalion of the 6th Iowa, formed his troops in a line of battle when they arrived at the ravine. He then discovered the 2nd Nebraska on his left flank, preparing to fight on foot. House's troops advanced, were fired on by the Indians, and returned the fire.[25]

Colonel David Wilson, commanding the First Battalion of the 6th Iowa, arrived at the ravine opposite the 2nd Nebraska and formed his troops parallel to the 2nd Nebraska line.

---

[22]Goodwin, p. 251; *Official Records*, p. 558.

[23]*Official Records*, p. 566.

[24]*Ibid.*

[25]*Ibid.*

While moving his troops forward, Wilson got "detached from the First and was thrown into the Third Battalion."[26] Wilson apparently led some of his troops into battle with empty weapons,[27] and during the battle his horse was shot out from under him.[28] Wilson stated the Indians started the battle by firing first.

After Sully had placed a guard around the Indian prisoners who surrendered, he positioned his troops and the battery, which was not used in the battle, on small hills near the Indian camp. The Second Battalion of the 6th Iowa was held in reserve during the engagement.[29]

---

[26]Drips, p. 44; *Official Records*, p. 562.

[27]Both Sgt. Drips and Pvt. Spencer mentioned the incident of the unloaded weapons. Drips wrote: "Some of the Sixth went into the ground with their arms unloaded, whose fault it was remains to be seen yet, as I do not lay blame to any one." Spencer wrote: "Just as we had all got our places, Colonel Wilson came up and took command of the third Battallion. He foolishly ordered the men to mount their horses, and then, without giving the order to load their pieces, he marched them up to within thirty feet of the enemy, one company with their rifles unloaded." Drips, p. 45; Goodwin, p. 251.

[28]In his report of the battle Wilson described the loss of his horse: "It was at this fire of the enemy, when riding some little distance in advance of the battalion, that my horse was shot with a slug, fatally wounding him. He lived long enough to carry me about 30 rods." A report of the battle in *Harper's Weekly* two months later mentions "Colonel Wilson, who narrowly escaped, his horse being killed under him while gallantly leading his regiment."

Sgt. Drips recorded this incident in a slightly different light: "Some times a small accident or occurence changes circumstances so as to bestow glory and renown where it does not belong and sometimes withholds true merit where it ought to be bestowed. As an illustration of the former at the White Stone Hill fight some historian writes that Col. Wilson led the charge in person until his horse was shot from under him when he mounted another horse and continued the charge till the Indians were totally routed and driven from the field. The fact was that as the Colonel was getting away from the fight a soldier dismounting touched the trigger of his gun with his heel. The gun was discharged, the bullet going through the stifle of Col. Wilson's horse and as a matter of course the horse was ruined." *Official Records*, p. 562; "The Sioux War," *Harper's Weekly* (October 31, 1863), p. 695; Drips, p. 56.

[29]*Official Records*, p. 560; Drips, p. 44.

Colonel David Wilson

Photo from State Historical Society of North Dakota

The shooting at the ravine continued for about one half hour[30] while darkness was setting in. The noise and confusion of the battle made the cavalry horses difficult to control, and many of the Indians were finally able to escape through the 6th Iowa line when the soldiers' horses became unmanageable.[31]

It then rapidly became so dark that Colonel Furnas became convinced that Major House's troops were firing into his men, mistaking them for Indians.[32] Darkness forced the cavalry to withdraw from the ravine, and the Indians were able to escape during the night.

Each of the cavalry commands camped separately that night, with the troops remaining ready in case of further fighting:

> We were ordered to lay on our arms, which we did until morning, but such an awful noise as was kept up during the night, the dogs howling, and the squaws squalling, there was not much chance to sleep. We put out a heavy picket guard and the different companies gathered up their dead and wounded as well as they could.[33]

---

[30]Drips, p. 45.

[31]"Whitestone Battlefield," pp. 14, 16; Drips, p. 56; Goodwin, p. 251.

[32]*Official Records*, p. 567.

[33]Drips, p. 45.

About 50 years after the battle at Whitestone Hill, an Indian pictograph of the battle was drawn by Richard Cottonwood, as directed by Takes-His-Shield. A photostatic copy of this pictograph is displayed in the Whitestone Battlefield Historic Site museum.

Photo from State Historical Society of North Dakota

An interpretation of this pictograph (summarized on pages 97 and 98) was later written by Rev. Beede.

Interpretation from Shimmin-Tveit Museum Forbes, ND

Sioux Pictograph of the Battle

The pictograph on page 96 presents the Sioux Indian tradition of the conflict at Whitestone Hill. It was drawn about 50 years after the battle by Richard Cottonwood, as directed by Takes-His-Shield who was apparently at Whitestone Hill in 1863. The following explanation of the pictograph, or "map-history," is summarized from an interpretation written by Rev. Aaron McGaffey Beede in 1932, almost 20 years after the pictograph was drawn. Beede served as an Episcopal missionary among the Sioux at Fort Yates in North Dakota for many years.

The explanation begins near the number "1" on the pictograph, beside the circle of tipis. The many Sioux heads show that Indian men, women and children were at the camp. They were on their autumn buffalo hunt and drying meat for the winter, as indicated by the jerked meat hanging from poles supported by forked posts near the tipis. The camp was in the broken prairie country beside a small lake. The lake is shown, along with lines indicating hill ridges and a sort of squarish table land.

The camp consisted of two groups of Sioux, one accustomed to war and to spears, and the other using only arrows. War scalps are drawn on the tops of the tipi poles of some tipis and these tipis are shown with spears, while other tipi poles have no scalps and are shown with arrows. The two groups of Sioux were so friendly that they are all shown camped in one circle, not in two circles.

A large army of mounted white soldiers suddenly swooped down upon the Sioux, with the horse tracks of white soldiers shown in an orderly array or pattern. The soldiers' attack is shown coming from the lower right corner of the map. Most of the Indians started to run away, fleeing in the direction opposite the army. A fleeing woman has hitched a travois to a horse which has no rider, and three children are crowded onto this travois.

Now the perspective changes on the pictograph to the opposite corner labeled with number "2". An Indian reading this large pictograph on the floor would typically walk around the map to the opposite corner.

A small lake or hilly rise is shown near the "2". A large part of the army is rushing, shown by hoof prints in well-formed order, to encircle the fleeing Indians and cut off their escape. A smaller number of soldiers pursues the fleeing Indians without killing any of them. An Indian woman catches a get-away horse, places an old woman in the saddle, and hitches her travois loaded with children to the horse. No one has been killed yet.

A column of troops turns down near the outside of the "2", chasing Indians who had gone that way. Another woman with a get-away horse, together with many other Indians, swings by a circular route back toward the "1". So far no one has been killed, and these Indians have not put up a fight or any type of defense.

Now the viewpoint changes to the number "3" area. The troopers have the Indians between them and are killing the Indians, but the Indians are not fighting: not one arrow is in the picture. The mark that looks something like "R" on the face means the person was killed, and the fact that 25 or 30 of these marks are present in this part of the pictograph indicates a slaughter of the Indians.

Now the story moves to the number "4" area of the map. After killing the Indians, a large number of soldiers went away, with their horse tracks crossing the ones made earlier. Some of the Indians escaped at this time, indicated by the faces with no marks showing that they were killed. Then darkness came, so that no eyes actually saw where the troopers went or where the Indians escaped. The only events shown in the picture are those that could been seen, and what happened after darkness set in could not be seen. No Indians had fired arrows or fought the soldiers in any way, according to the pictograph.

Beede also wrote that he had once asked Takes-His-Shield why he was not in the map, as is usually the case with the Indian who makes the pictograph. According to Beede, Takes-His-Shield "said that since that time he had been in the other life . . . the same as dead, and so he must not put himself into it. There was a slight tremble in his voice, but other wise no emotion, firm set face and jaws . . . . He was a man of few words, & seldom talked with people about this matter."

It should be noted that as a historical source, this depiction of the Whitestone Hill conflict is only as accurate as the memory of one participant a half century after the event occurred, plus the still later interpretation by someone who was not there at all. The pictograph is valuable, however, because it does present the Indian tradition of the engagement.

The Scene the Next Day

The scene of the battlefield and Indian camp the next day was recorded by F.E. Caldwell, a soldier with the 2nd Nebraska Cavalry, as he remembered it almost 40 years later:

> Tepees, some standing, some torn down, some squaws that were dead, some that were wounded and still alive, young children of all ages from young infants to 8 or 10 years old, who had lost their parents, dead soldiers, dead Indians, dead horses, hundreds of dogs howling for their masters. Some of the dogs were packed with small poles fastened to a collar and dragging behind them. On the poles was a platform on which all kinds of articles were fastened on – in one instance a young baby.[34]

Col. Furnas, in his journal, also described the scene on September 4:

> The whole country for miles was covered with roving howling dogs, and ponies. The Indians fled leaving *everything*, tents, meat, cooking utensils, and 15 or 20 small children. . . . We camped for the day on the ground occupied by the Indians when they were discovered.[35]

Reports of the casualties of the cavalry vary, but it has become generally accepted that 20 soldiers died as a result of the engagement and 38 were wounded. These figures include two soldiers who were killed while on a scouting party on September 5. Some of the soldiers were killed outright during the battle and some died from serious wounds a short time

---

[34]"Whitestone Battlefield," p. 14.

[35]Rowen, p. 24.

later. Between 600 and 700 troops were engaged in the battle.[36]

Indian casualties from the battle can only be estimated because their bodies were scattered over a wide area. Some of the Indians killed in the fighting were probably carried from the battle site by other Indians during the night. Some of the wounded may have died at a later time and place. Sully estimated the number of Indians killed at 100, and then went on to add: "My officers and the guides I have with me think 150 will not cover their loss. The Indian reports make it over 200." Drips estimated the Indian casualties at "300 killed and wounded." In addition to the dead and wounded, 156 Indians were taken prisoner: 32 men and 124 women and children.[37]

On the morning following the battle, Sully established his camp at the site of the abandoned Indian camp.[38] Troops were sent out to look for the Indians who had fled and to round up horses, mules and ponies.

The cavalry scouting parties did not engage the Indians in battle again until September 5, however. At that time a 27-man detachment led by Lt. Charles Hall ran into about 300 Indians several miles from the camp. Two soldiers were killed by the Indians and the rest were "so closely pressed by the enemy that the men increased the rapidity of their retreat, without orders."[39]

---

[36]*Official Records*, p. 561; Drips, p. 46.

[37]*Official Records*, pp. 560-61; Drips, p. 45.

[38]Drips, p. 46.

[39]*Official Records*, p. 611.

Destroying Everything Left Behind

The most severe defeat for the Indians came not from the battle itself, but from the destruction that followed. The soldiers destroyed their food and equipment, as described by Caldwell:

> Sully ordered all the property destroyed, tepees, buffalo skins, and all their things, including tons and tons of dried buffalo meat and tallow. It was gathered in wagons, piled in a hollow and burned, and the melted tallow ran down that valley in a stream. Hatchets, camp kettles and all things that would sink were thrown into a small lake.[40]

Estimates of the amount of dried buffalo meat destroyed range widely, but the figures 400,000 to 500,000 pounds probably come as close as any.[41] This supply of meat "represented more than one thousand slaughtered buffalo."[42] Drips described the quantity of meat destroyed in another way:

> The defeat of the Indians was the worse from the fact that they had made this camp on purpose to put up their winter's meat and the season being pretty well over they had a very large quantity on hand, all of which was destroyed. To show the extent of their loss in a measure I will just say that it took a party of 100 men two days to gather up the stuff and burn it.[43]

---

[40]"Whitestone Battlefield," p. 14.

[41]The wide range of estimates of the amount of dried buffalo meat destroyed is not surprising since such a large quantity was involved. Sully estimated 400,000 to 500,000 pounds. House placed the amount at 400 tons, which would be 800,000 pounds. Spencer said about 100 tons (200,000 pounds). Sully's estimate has the advantage of being the median amount of these three. Sully, being an officer of considerable experience, was also probably able to estimate more accurately than the younger men.

[42]Clement A. Lounsberry, *North Dakota, History and People* (Chicago: S.J. Clarke Publishing Co., 1917), p. 290.

[43] Drips, pp. 45-46.

The soldiers buried many of their dead on a knoll near the Indian camp on September 5.[44] Sgt. Drips recalled that:

The fatigue squad was busy all day in burying the dead and in burning up the Indian stuff, part of which was piled on the graves of our lost comrades and burnt in order to keep the vandals from despoiling the last resting place of the departed.[45]

Cpl. Pierce of the 2nd Nebraska Cavalry also summarized the destruction of Indian property on September 5:

---

[44]Most firsthand accounts of the battle do not specifically mention the burial of the soldiers. Drips, however, provides some interesting insight into this matter, particularly in the case of Lieutenant Leavitt's grave.

Lieut. Thomas J. Leavitt of Company B, 6th Iowa Cavalry, was mortally wounded, but not killed outright, during the battle on Sept. 3rd. On the 5th two soldiers, Quartermaster Sergeant Rodgers and Private Killsa, were killed while on a scouting party. A detail sent out later on the 5th recovered the body of Rodgers but could not find that of Killsa. This detail returned to camp around 8 p.m.

When the expedition left Whitestone Hill on the 6th, they "had along the remains of Lieut. Leavitt and Sergeant Rodgers." They headed in a southerly direction and marched about 18 miles. In the evening they "deposited the remains of Sergeant Rodgers and another soldier from Company G in their last resting place, right under the horse line to fool the Indians. This man from Company G died on the march today." The man from Company G buried with Rodgers appears to have been Private Stephens.

Drips does not indicate that Lieut. Leavitt was buried with the other two men that evening, nor does he mention the officer's burial in following entries in his diary. It therefore seems highly probable that Lieut. Leavitt was buried sometime during the march that day (between Whitestone Hill and the camp site 18 miles to the south).

Many years ago an unidentified soldier's grave was discovered by local farmers seven miles south of Whitestone Hill. This was concluded to have been the grave of an officer because it contained a silk handkerchief and other accessories of an officer's uniform. It appears highly probable that this was the grave of Lieut. Leavitt.

Maps showing the military campaigns in Dakota Territory do not indicate that any other expeditions passed through this area. This would also seem to indicate that the officer buried seven miles south of Whitestone Hill had been a member of Sully's expedition. Lieut. Leavitt was the only officer who died as a result of the battle of Whitestone Hill. Drips, p. 48; and information supplied by Iver Tveit, Forbes, ND.

[45]Drips, p. 47.

This sketch of the Battle of Whitestone Hill appeared in *Harper's Weekly* on October 31, 1863. Gen. Sully, an artist as well as an officer, recorded the same scene in a painting. This picture does not accurately depict the battle, however, since the actual fighting occurred in a ravine about one-half mile from the Indian camp.

103

I don't think there ever had been a battle so fierce & destructive to any one tribe as this, we captured a good many of their ponies, all that they needed to make themselves comfortable such as tools for tanning their hides, beads, paints, porcupine quills & trinkets of every name & shape . . . buffalo jerk meat, tens of thousands of pounds nice sweet & good was consigned to the flames & their property kettles, dishes, robes & trinkets . . . went on to the same pile.[46]

Sully's expedition left the Whitestone Hill camp on September 6 and headed south toward Fort Pierre along the Missouri River. The 156 Indian prisoners were taken along and placed on the Crow Creek reservation that had been established along the Missouri River in the spring of 1863.[47]

Severe Consequences

Although Sully's expedition had been delayed along the Missouri and therefore arrived too late to trap the Indians in the pincer movement with Sibley's troops as planned, it was nevertheless considered a success by the military. Sully believed that he had dealt the Indians camped at Whitestone Hill "one of the most severe punishments that the Indians have ever received."[48] Pope, in a letter written October 5, congratulated Sully:

The results are entirely satisfactory, and I doubt not that the effect upon the Northwestern Indians will be, as you report, of the highest consequence. Whilst I regret that difficulties and obstacles of a serious character prevented your co-operation with General Sibley at the time hoped, I bear willing testimony to

---

[46]Rowen, pp. 48-49.

[47]Zena Irma Trinka, *Out Where the West Begins* (St. Paul: The Pioneer Company, 1920), p. 73.

[48]*Official Records,* p. 559.

the distinguished conduct of yourself and your command.[49]

In November, 1863, Sam Brown, a 19-year-old interpreter at Crow Creek, presented the Indian side of Sully's battle at Whitestone Hill in a letter to his father:

> I hope you will not believe all that is said of "Sullys' Successfull Expedition," against the Sioux. I don't think he aught to brag of it at all, because it was, what no decent man would have done, he pitched into their camp and just slaughtered them, worse a great deal than what the Indians did in 1862, he killed *very few* men and took *no* hostile ones prisoners ... and now he returns saying that we need fear no more, for he has "wiped out all hostile Indians from Dakota." If he had killed men instead of women & children, then it would have been a success, and the worse of it, they had no hostile intention whatever, the Nebraska 2nd pitched into them without orders, while the Iowa 6th were shaking hands with them on one side, they even shot their own men.[50]

The campaigns by Sibley and Sully in 1863 were concentrated in eastern Dakota Territory, an area that had long been the homeland of the Yanktonai and Hunkpatina tribes. The consequences for these Indians were severe; some were killed, some were escorted to the Crow Creek reservation as prisoners, and those who escaped at Whitestone Hill lost their personal property as well as their principal food supply for the winter. In addition, these Indians became more aware of the disastrous effects that might accompany any future attempt to resist white control. The expeditions of 1863 were the last campaigns conducted east of the Missouri River.

---

[49]*Correspondence*, p. 608.

[50]Sam J. Brown to Joseph R. Brown, November 13, 1863, Joseph Brown Papers (Archives, Minnesota Historical Society, St. Paul).

Chapter 8

Road to Reservations

Settlers, government officials, and other citizens on the frontier continued to put pressure on the military for a more decisive settlement of the Indian situation in Dakota Territory. In 1863 the Yankton *Dakotaian* wrote that it expected Sully to return from his campaign "with scalps enough to carpet Pennsylvania avenue from the president's mansion to the capitol." John Hutchinson, the acting governor of Dakota Territory, was among those favoring another campaign in 1864, and stated that "these Hostile tribes must be conquered, and must be compelled to make new treaties, before there will be any safety to the white man within this superintendency."[1]

During the winter of 1863-64, Pope planned an expedition west of the Missouri River for the following summer. Sully was placed in charge of a force of about 2,200 troops from Iowa, Minnesota and Dakota. He traveled up the Missouri River and selected a spot south of present day Mandan, North Dakota, for the construction of Fort Rice. From there Sully

---

[1]Richard N. Ellis, "Civilians, the Army and the Indian Problem on the Northern Plains, 1862-1866," *North Dakota History*, 37-1 (Winter, 1970), pp. 24-25.

started west on July 19, 1864, having learned earlier from some Yanktonais who had been at the Whitestone Hill battle the previous year that about 1,600 lodges of Sioux were "near the head of the Heart River or on the Little Missouri."[2] Sully's troops were also escorting an immigrant train headed for Idaho.

Battle at Killdeer Mountain

On July 23 Sully turned north toward the Knife River, and five days later his troops found the Indians at Killdeer Mountain (also referred to as *Tahkahokuty* Mountain). Sully described the terrain as "a small chain of very high hills, filled with ravines, thickly timbered and well watered, situated on a branch of the Little Missouri." Sully estimated that there were "at least 5,000 or 6,000 warriors, composed of the Unkpapas, Sans Arcs, Blackfeet, Minneconjous, Yanktonais, and Santee Sioux," but historian Doane Robinson said that Sully's estimate was greatly exaggerated and that the Indians claimed there were about 1,600 men at Killdeer Mountain.[3]

Sully's troops, aided by their battery, succeeded in dislodging the Indians from their positions in the rugged terrain, and also forced them to desert much of the property at their campsite. Estimates of the number of Indians killed vary from 31 to more than 100. On the following day, July 29, troops under Colonel Robert McLaren destroyed the Indian property at the campsite:

The men gathered into heaps and burned tons of dried buffalo meat packed in buffalo skin cases, great quantities of dried berries, buffalo robes, tanned buffalo,

---

[2]Louis Pfaller, "Sully's Expedition of 1864: Killdeer Mountain and Badlands Battles," *North Dakota History*, 31-1 (January, 1964), pp. 34-35.

[3]*War of the Rebellion*, Vol. XLI, Part I – Reports, p. 142; Doane Robinson, p. 334.

The Battle
at Killdeer
Mountain
in Dakota
Territory,
July 28,
1864.

Painting
by Carl L.
Boeckmann

*Photo from
Minnesota
Historical
Society*

elk, and antelope skins, household utensils, such as brass and copper kettles, mess pans, &c., riding saddles, dray poles for ponies and dogs.

Finding that one day was too short a time to make the destruction complete, I ordered the men to gather only the lodge poles in heaps and burn them, and then deployed the men and fired the woods in every direction; the destruction was thus complete.[4]

After the battle at Killdeer Mountain, Sully returned to the Heart River and headed west toward the Yellowstone River. This route took the expedition through the Badlands of what is today western North Dakota. In this rugged country, which Sully described as "Hell with the fires put out,"[5] the troops skirmished with the Indians again. After reaching the Yellowstone River on August 12, the soldiers followed it to the Missouri and began their return trip down the river. On September 11, Sully reported to Pope that "the expedition ... has been a success in every respect as far as it was in the power of any one or any body of troops to make it so."[6]

On October 26, 1864, John Pell, the commander at Fort Sully, wrote to General Sully concerning the possibilities of making peace with the Yanktonais:

I regard that portion of the Yanktonais under Medicine Bear as more uncertain than any other, as they have been tampered with by the traders of the north and offered munitions of war and a city of refuge in the British Possessions. Two Bears says he can make peace for the whole tribe, but I am afraid he is somewhat of an Indian braggart, as he has only about forty lodges, while Bone Necklace has about the same number in the friendly camp, and Medicine Bear has

---

[4]*War of the Rebellion*, Vol. XLI, Part I, pp. 143, 172; Doane Robinson, p. 334.
[5]Drips, p. 81; Pfaller, p. 58.
[6]*War of the Rebellion*, Vol. XLI, Part I, p. 154.

over 100. Yet still I believe he also will come in when he finds himself standing alone among all the Indians.

Pell went on to state that "their severe punishment in life and property for the last two years is an excellent groundwork for a peace that I believe would be lasting if they could . . . be treated with justice and humanity instead of being preyed upon by a horde of Indian traders and speculators."[7]

Negotiating Treaties

During the early 1860's a conflict had developed in Dakota Territory between military and civilian authorities over who should have control of Indian affairs. Dakota Territorial Governor Newton Edmunds and other government officials wanted to negotiate a peace treaty, including annuity payments, with the Sioux. Military officials, including Pope and Sully, opposed "these bribing treaties" and from past experience knew that they would lead to hostilities which the army would be ordered to suppress. The military wanted sole jurisdiction over the Indians and wanted peace treaties that did not involve either money or goods:

Pope was convinced that the present policy with its attraction to the worst elements of white society – the whiskey seller and the crooked Indian agents and traders – would soon wipe this once proud race from the face of the earth. Grant was in basic agreement regarding this class of citizens and wrote: "It may be the Indians require as much protection from the whites as the whites do from the Indians."[8]

---

[7]*War of the Rebellion*, Vol. LIII – Reports, Correspondence, Etc., p. 601.

[8]Ellis, "Civilians, the Army and the Indian Problem on the Northern Plains," pp. 29, 34-36.

Governor Edmunds and the peace faction won out in 1865, and negotiated treaties with a number of bands along the Missouri River. Among the Indians who signed a treaty for the Hunkpapa at Fort Sully on October 20, 1865, were three Yanktonai chiefs: Two Bears, White Bear and Bone Necklace.[9] It was not explained why three Yanktonai chiefs signed a treaty supposedly made with the Hunkpapa tribe of the Teton division.

The commissioners, headed by Edmunds, negotiated a similar treaty with the "Yanktonai band" at Fort Sully on October 20, and Two Bears was again among the signers. On October 28 a treaty was made with the "Upper Yanktonai band" at Fort Sully. Big Head, Little Soldier and Black Catfish were among the Yanktonai chiefs to sign this treaty.

In these treaties, the Indians agreed to cease all hostilities against United States citizens and against members of other tribes. They also agreed to withdraw from overland routes through their territory. In return, the Yanktonai band was to receive an annuity of $30 per lodge for 20 years, and the Upper Yanktonai band was to get $10,000 annually for 25 years. Indians who chose to take up agriculture were promised annual assistance in the form of agricultural implements and improvements.[10]

Following these treaties, the commissioners announced that they had made peace with more than 16,000 Sioux and that the Indian war was over. The commissioners had made little effort to contact the hostiles, however, and "the Indians who did sign the agreements were those whom the hostiles derisively termed 'stay around the fort' people."[11] It was clear that the commissioners had failed to make peace with the

---

[9]Kappler, p. 902; Anderson, p. 34.

[10]Kappler, pp. 903-06.

[11]Ellis, "Civilians, the Army and the Indian Problem on the Northern Plains," pp. 37-38.

entire Sioux nation when the Red Cloud War broke out in opposition to the Bozeman Trail in 1866.

While the 1865 treaties included a significant portion of the Yanktonais, not all of them attended the peace conferences. (A few who later moved farther west were at the Indian camp on the Little Big Horn River at the time of the famous battle with Lt. Col. Custer in 1876.[12]) The campaigns through Yanktonai territory in 1863 and west of the Missouri in 1864 had, however, convinced many of them of the necessity of avoiding war with the whites. These Indians lived east of the Missouri and followed the military regulations which limited their hunting territory despite food shortages which they experienced during the 1865-66 winter.[13]

On June 5, 1867, General Sully and General Ely Parker met with some of the Yanktonai leaders at Crow Creek, and these chiefs talked about being given reservations east of the Missouri River. Bone Necklace, White Bear, Running Bear and Two Bears were among the Yanktonais at this meeting.[14]

In 1868 the United States government did negotiate a treaty which included a reservation for the Yanktonais, but this reservation was west of the Missouri and was known as the "Great Sioux Reservation."[15]

The Great Sioux Reservation

The Great Sioux Reservation was created on the basis of findings by a commission appointed in early 1867. The members of this commission were to investigate the causes of Sioux hostilities, including the Oglala attack in which Captain William J. Fetterman and the 80 men with him were killed, and

---

[12]Doane Robinson, p. 433.

[13]Anderson, pp. 33-34.

[14]*Ibid.*, p. 34.

[15]Hurt, *Sioux Indians II*, p. 233.

to gather information for a potential Sioux reservation at the same time. Reports were filed by several of the commissioners, and the recommendations made by John B. Sanborn were substantially accepted by Congress.[16]

> Sanborn recommended the abandonment of aggressive war, the restoration of friendly relations, and the establishment of the Sioux on a large reservation, with the eventual aim of teaching them to be self-supporting in the white man's economy. As an alternative, Sanborn pointed out that "it would probably require from five to ten years" for a force of 25,000 men "to conquer a peace" at an expense of probably "from three to four hundred millions of dollars."[17]

In July 1867, Congress created another commission with the authority to negotiate treaties which would include a reservation to serve as a permanent home for the Indians. The commission held a series of meetings with various groups of Sioux in 1867 and 1868, and at the council at Fort Rice on July 2, 1868, the Lower Yanktonai chief Two Bears voiced his objections to the reservation proposal:

> Now I will tell you one thing that I don't like; you are going to put all the tribes together and I do not approve of it. I speak for my own band; our country is on the other side of the river – we are Yanctonais .... The trouble was begun by the whites rushing into our country .... There is one thing that I must tell you: though I want to make peace, yet I don't want to sell my land to the whites. It is the whites who will break the treaty not us. I don't give permission to any white men to chop wood and get hay in our country.[18]

---

[16]Richard N. Ellis, *General Pope and U.S. Indian Policy* (Albuquerque: University of New Mexico Press, 1970), pp. 124-25; Anderson, pp. 44-45.

[17]Anderson, p. 45.

[18]*Ibid.*, p. 38.

Two Bears, Yanktonai Chief

Photo from State Historical Society of North Dakota

The peace commission succeeded in gaining the approval of the 1868 treaty by portions of the Arapaho and of ten different Sioux tribes: the Brule, Oglala, Miniconjou, Hunkpapa, Blackfeet, Two Kettle, Sans Arcs, Santee, Yanktonai and Cuthead Sioux. Among the chiefs to sign for the Yanktonais were Two Bears, Little Soldier, Black Eye, Black Catfish and Medicine Bear. Big Head was among those to sign for the Cutheads.[19]

The Great Sioux Reservation outlined in the 1868 treaty was bounded by the Missouri River on the east, the northern boundary of Nebraska on the south, the 104th degree of west longitude on the west (the present western boundary of the Dakotas), and the 46th parallel of latitude on the north (slightly north of the present North and South Dakota border).[20] It covered an area of over 40,000 square miles, consisting primarily of the western half of present day South Dakota.

In addition to establishing a reservation for the Sioux, the 1868 treaty contained a number of other provisions. The United States would provide a physician, carpenter, miller, engineer, farmer, teachers and blacksmiths for the reservation each year. Each Indian would be given a suit of clothing annually for thirty years, and each Indian over four years old would receive "one pound of meat and one pound of flour per day" for four years. The Indians agreed "to compel their children, male and female, between the ages of six and sixteen years, to attend school."[21]

The United States agreed "that the country north of the North Platte River and east of the summits of the Big Horn Mountains" would be considered "unceded Indian territory," and that the military posts there would be abandoned and the

---

[19]Kappler, pp. 98, 105, 107.

[20]Bert Glen Pipal, "A History of Standing Rock Indian Agency, 1868-1880" (Unpublished Master's thesis, State University of South Dakota, 1962), p. 6; Kappler, p. 998.

[21]Kappler, pp. 1000-02.

road through this territory closed. The Indians reserved the right "to hunt on any lands north of North Platte, and on the Republican Fork of the Smoky Hill River, so long as the buffalo may range thereon in such numbers as to justify the chase."[22] This portion of the treaty was considered a victory for the Sioux who had objected to the forts and to the Bozeman Trail during the Red Cloud War.

The treaty contained a number of provisions to induce the Indians to farm. Any Indian wishing to farm could select up to 320 acres on the reservation and claim it as his own as long as he continued to cultivate it. Indians who took up farming would receive seeds and agricultural implements for three years, and each family that chose to farm would receive "one good American cow, and one good well-broken pair of American oxen." The treaty even provided that $500 in presents would be given annually to the ten Indians who, in the agent's judgment, grew the most valuable crops that year.[23]

Three agencies were established along the Missouri River in 1869 to handle the affairs of the Indians on the Great Sioux Reservation. These were the Grand River Agency (moved and renamed Standing Rock in 1874), the Whetstone Agency (renamed Spotted Tail in 1874), and the Cheyenne River Agency.[24] The agencies and reservations east of the Missouri, including Crow Creek and Devils Lake, were also available for Indians included under the 1868 treaty.[25] Although the Indians were not confined to specific reservations after the treaty, they were encouraged, and to a certain extent forced, to settle on the reservations in the years that followed.

---

[22]Kappler, pp.1002-03.

[23]*Ibid.*, pp. 999-1002.

[24]Edward E. Hill, *The Office of Indian Affairs, 1824-1880: Historical Sketches* (New York: Clearwater Publishing Company, 1974), p. 58.

[25]Kappler, p. 998.

The members of the Yanktonai division of the Sioux settled on four separate reservations. The Yanktonai proper or Upper Yanktonais were chiefly on the Standing Rock Reservation in North Dakota. The Hunkpatina or Lower Yanktonais settled mainly on the Crow Creek Reservation in South Dakota, and some also lived on the Standing Rock Reservation in North Dakota. Most of the *Pabaksa* or Cutheads settled on the Devils Lake Reservation in North Dakota. And many Yanktonais, often designated as Yanktons, settled on the Fort Peck Reservation in Montana.[26]

Drifting Goose Village

While other bands of the Yanktonai division were being settled on reservations created for them by the government, one group of Hunkpatinas remained in their tribal homeland of eastern Dakota Territory. The members of this village, under Chief Drifting Goose, lived in permanent earthlodges along the James River (near present day Melette, South Dakota). These Indians had been at Whitestone Hill when Sully's troops attacked the camp in 1863. Their earthlodge village and the surrounding land which they farmed had later been designated as a reserve for them.[27]

In 1880, however, an executive order classified the Drifting Goose reserve as public domain and opened the area to white settlement. The Indians from the reserve were transferred to the Crow Creek Reservation.[28] With the removal of the Drifting Goose band, the last of the Yanktonais left their long occupied homeland east of the Missouri River in Dakota Territory and moved onto government created reservations.

---

[26]J.W. Powell, "Indian Linguistic Families," in *Seventh Annual Report of the Bureau of Ethnology, 1885-'86* (Washington: Government Printing Office, 1891), p. 115; Hodge, p. 991; Curtis, p. 122; Howard, "Middle Dakota," p. 9.

[27]Milligan, p. 21; Howard, "Drifting Goose's Village," p. 2.

[28]Milligan, p. 99.

Indian reservations established in Dakota Territory in the late 1860's opened the way for white settlement on the prairies where the buffalo and the Yanktonai Sioux had flourished. By the 1880's, towns were appearing where Indian villages once stood, and plows were rapidly burying the native buffalo grass.

The battle at Whitestone Hill was the pivotal encounter in a cultural clash in eastern Dakota Territory. The traditional Indian way of life was being replaced by white settlements and farms on the frontier. When these two widely differing cultures clashed, there was no compromise solution.

In 1942 a plaque was erected at the Whitestone Hill Battlefield Historic Site in memory of the Indians who were there in 1863. Alberta Two Bears (standing in front), a descendant of Chief Two Bears, unveiled the plaque. From left to right are Agnes Looking Horse, James All Yellow, Basil Two Bears (grandson of Two Bears), Mrs. Basil Two Bears, and Frank Young Bear.

Photo from
Shimmin-Tveit Museum,
Forbes, North Dakota